Holly Bell

Power of Frozen

Cook Book

Iceland

Holly Bell

Power of Frozen

Cook Book

Iceland

First published in Great Britain by Jon Croft Editions in 2015.

Jon Croft Editions
Scarborough House
29 James Street West
Bath, BA1 2BT

info@joncrofteditions.com
www.joncrofteditions.com

Publisher Jon Croft
Commissioning Editor Meg Avent
Editor Eleanor van Zandt
Proofreader Gillian Haslam
Indexer Ruth Ellis
Photographer Mike Cooper
Photographer's Assistant Alex Shore
Cover Photography Scott Choucino
Art Director and Designer Kim Musgrove
Food Stylist Holly Bell
Prop Stylist Jaine Bevan
Hair and Make-Up Katy Short

Printed in Slovenia on behalf of Latitude Press.

Contents

A huge part of this book is about getting families to have fun with food and enjoy eating together. That is why Iceland is proud to be donating the profits of this book to the Children's Food Trust.

The Children's Food Trust is a national charity whose vision is that all children have a balanced diet, the cooking skills and food education they need for good health and to reach their potential. To see details of their fantastic work visit www.childrensfoodtrust.org.uk

Quite simply, when children eat better, they do better.

Happy cooking!

Children's Food Trust registered charity number 1118995

Introduction

 Everybody needs a reliable recipe book of family staples, full of tasty, economical and easy-to-prepare meal ideas that get you through the week – so that at the weekend you're ready to take on recipes that require a little more time and effort. This is exactly that book and I've written it to celebrate Iceland's 45th birthday.

I've divided the recipes into chapters reflecting how I search for recipes myself. Sometimes I just want a light lunch or a starter; at other times I'm looking for easy mid-week suppers, requiring minimal hands-on time, when the temptation to phone for a takeaway is high after a busy day with work or the kids.

Then there are those occasions when only comfort food will do. And, of course, there are times when we all want to push the boat out, by creating food that's impressive and really special, but without spending the whole day in the kitchen. Lastly, there's a chapter of cakes, bakes and puddings – well, I couldn't write a recipe book without some sweet treats to finish off a meal, could I?

I hope you enjoy making these recipes as much as I do. So many are recipes that have existed only in my head until now, others are dishes I enjoyed as a child years ago and now my boys, in turn, also love. At last they're all written down in one place; I hope they'll become your family favourites as well.

Holly Bell
x

Iceland

Why I Love My Freezer

My freezer is basically my main store cupboard reserve. It's big enough to supply a family of five but, being an upright model, not so big that it takes up too much space (although I do secretly long for a chest freezer). I love frozen food for so many reasons. For one thing, it means less waste; and boy, do I hate waste! Like so many of us, I work to a weekly food budget and can't bear to throw anything away. Using frozen food, whether bought or homemade, enables me to use only what I need. It allows me to grab a healthy and nutritious meal at short notice – often stowed away months in advance – with which to feed my family well.

Now that there are five of us to feed, I appreciate how economical frozen food is and I especially like that it's often fresher than 'fresh' food. The fish is frozen at sea, rather than being frozen and then defrosted to sit on a fish counter. The vegetables are frozen after picking, too, rather than sitting in warehouses and lorries, their nutritional quality deteriorating as they make their journey to our shopping baskets.

I also like that frozen food, being so often frozen at the source, gives me access to treats I usually get to savour only on holiday. Fish from far shores and gelato straight from the continent are regularly enjoyed at my house, although obviously it's a little colder and swimwear is rarely worn!

Of course, freezing food to preserve it requires no nasty artificial preservatives or extra sugar and salt. The cold does a fine job of preserving on its own, which makes me feel very happy about feeding my children frozen food. It tastes good, maintains nutrients, helps me manage my weekly budget and gives my family access to food and flavours from all over the world. What's not to like?

Freezer Husbandry

Freezer husbandry (my term for the art of maintaining and using a freezer to feed your family) need not mean charts and lists of what's in each drawer. It doesn't even need to involve colour coding. I think whoever is doing the lion's share of the family cooking tends to know what they have in their freezer, fridge and cupboards. It's like a sixth sense. If you don't, and the freezer feels disorganised – an icy abyss of unidentified frozen objects – then a simple system of keeping separate drawers for meat, fish, vegetables, sweet treats, homemade and/or bought 'ready' meals and family staples works well. Lastly, keeping a drawer for those nifty little extras that make creating delicious meals that bit easier is worth the investment in time and effort.

These extras are those little bits of magic you can add to your freezer, week by week, that will make all the difference to that risotto, gravy or daily lunchbox menu, or simply help answer the perennial question 'What's for pudding?' Here are some ideas to stow away in your freezer for a (not so) rainy day:

Breakfast

- Breakfast muffins (savoury ones) freeze really well and can be left out to defrost overnight, or simply heated through (from frozen, in the original baking tin) in an oven preheated to 200°C/Fan 180°C/Gas Mark 6 for about 20 minutes.

- Pretty much everyone loves pancakes, but the recipe often makes more than you need. Stow the uneaten ones in the freezer between pieces of non-stick baking paper.

- Potato pancakes also freeze well; to make them just mix together 140g plain mashed potato, 40g self-raising flour, 40ml milk, 20g melted butter, 1 teaspoon bicarbonate of soda, 1 teaspoon salt and 1 teaspoon freshly ground black pepper and form into patties; fry in a little butter and olive oil until brown on each side and serve as an accompaniment to the great British fry-up.

Iceland

Mains

- Homemade burgers and meatballs (housing various types of cheese in the centre) are great freezer staples. Homemade ones taste so special and can be personalised with chilli, chorizo, garlic or herbs. If you make them in batches they're pretty speedy. Just remember to open-freeze meatballs on a baking tray before bagging. To do this, lay them on a tray lined with non-stick baking paper so they don't touch, then once frozen solid put them in a suitable freezer bag or freezer-proof container to avoid freezer burn (where food takes on a leathery thick skin from being exposed to the cold for too long) and place them back in the freezer until frozen. Separate burgers with non-stick baking paper before freezing.

- Homemade tomato sauce is a freezer lifesaver. Simmer 1 chopped onion, 1 x 400g can chopped tomatoes, 2 tablespoons tomato purée, 2 peeled and crushed garlic cloves, 1 teaspoon salt and 2 tablespoons olive oil on a low heat for about 30 minutes until thick and cooked down. Freeze in small bags, then flatten (they defrost much more quickly this way), and use as a pizza sauce, in pasta, on chicken breasts with a little cheese on top or as the base for a curry.

- There are always a few 'pizza kits' in my freezer – homemade pizza dough rolled into a ball and bagged, a container of sweet, smooth tomato sauce and some grated cheese. Simply defrost the dough and sauce, make your pizza and use the cheese from frozen.

Sides

- Homemade Yorkshire puddings add a bit of roast dinner comfort to a Monday night dinner. Make a batch and freeze in bags. Reheat from frozen for 5–10 minutes in the oven until warmed through.

- Did you know that you can make your own frozen roast potatoes and cook them straight from the freezer? Parboil your potatoes, drain and toss in salt, pepper and either a tablespoon of plain flour or polenta, drizzle with olive oil and open-freeze (see left). Once frozen, bag up. Roast from frozen at 220°C/Fan 200°C/Gas Mark 7 for 1 hour until crisp and brown.

- Jacket potatoes take some time to bake in the oven until the skin is really crunchy, so when the oven's on bake a few and freeze them for another day. They can be baked from frozen at 200°C/Fan 180°C/Gas Mark 6 for 20 minutes or 5 minutes per potato in the microwave. Check that they're piping hot before serving.

Iceland

Desserts and Sweet Treats

- Smoothie lollies are a healthy, but not too worthy finish to a meal. Just whizz up frozen berries with natural yoghurt and a little honey and freeze in lolly moulds.

- Meringues freeze like a dream and defrost in 10 minutes (though you can also munch on them frozen). Mix broken meringue pieces, whipped double cream and fresh red fruit as a low-effort, quick Eton mess, or use a meringue nest for a more polished creation. You can also stir meringue crumbs, a few broken digestives and lemon curd through vanilla ice cream for a quick, but special, lemon meringue pie ice cream.

- From November onwards I keep a few batches of mince pies in the freezer, taking just a few out at a time. That way they're fresh, I'm less likely to gobble them all up, and if an unexpected visitor arrives I can offer them a warm pie by baking it in a preheated oven at 200°C/Fan 180°C/Gas Mark 6 from frozen (in the original baking tin) for about 20 minutes. Serve with orange or brandy-laced butter.

- When making a crumble I make loads of the crumble mixture so I've some left for freezing. This basic recipe feeds four people but can be scaled up or down as needed: rub 100g butter into 120g plain flour and stir in 60g caster sugar. Freeze the excess in bags, then simply use from frozen. Make some regular and some with oats or chopped nuts.

- I keep a few 'naked' cupcakes in the freezer. A batch of 12 is too much for us to get through, and having a few un-iced ones means we're always half an hour away from a fun (if messy) cake-decorating morning with my sons and their pals.

- Freeze pieces of cake, brownies and flapjacks in individual portions for the dual use of providing cake for lunchboxes and keeping the rest of the contents cold. Just remove at breakfast and they'll be defrosted by lunchtime.

Magical Extra Ingredients

- After roasting a joint or a whole chicken, you'll have some bones or a whole carcass left over. If you want to make stock, you can simply freeze the bones in bags until the stock-making mood strikes you.

- Any bread past its best can be whizzed in the food processor and frozen in bags to use straight from the freezer for coating fishcakes, adding to meatballs or making into breadcrumb ice cream.

- Many recipes require a mirepoix as a base for flavour; this is a mixture of fresh, finely chopped onions, celery and carrots. You can make this in large batches and open freeze it, then tip it into bags to use from frozen.

- When frozen in ice cube portions, harissa (a heady, aromatic paste of chilli and spices) is a great 5-minute marinade that can be defrosted quickly in the microwave and rubbed into chicken or pork. Just soak 10 dried chillies in warm water for an hour, then drain and blend with 5 peeled garlic cloves, 1 teaspoon salt, 30ml olive oil and ½ teaspoon each of ground coriander and ground cumin.

- Roasted garlic is sweeter and less harsh in flavour than the raw cloves and will add depth to stews and sauces. The next time the oven's on, roast whole heads of garlic, then, once cool, squeeze the oozy garlic cloves out into the compartments of an ice cube tray and freeze.

- Make patties of flavoured butters to fry meat in, melt over vegetables, spread on bread and scones or use on oven-baked fish. Try one or more of the following: garlic, chilli, lemon zest, parsley, caramelised onions, pesto, sundried tomatoes, mustard seeds, fried bacon, lime zest, orange zest, vanilla extract, brandy or honey. There are so many combinations to try! Just chop your chosen ingredients into tiny pieces, mash with softened butter and shape into individual patties and freeze.

Iceland

• If you have any leftover fresh herbs, don't let them wilt and waste away; you can freeze them, chopped, in olive oil, in ice cube trays. Store in bags and use from frozen.

• Make a vat of caramelised sliced onions by slow-frying with oil, salt and a pinch of sugar, then freeze in ice cube trays for throwing into pasta dishes, mashed potato, curries and gravy.

• Nuts are prone to going rancid at room temperature so store in the freezer if you find you never use a full bag.

• Parmesan and Grana Padano rinds may not be good for grating, but they're perfect for adding body and flavour to soups and risottos as they bubble away. I freeze the rinds as they're discarded, so I always have a bag in the freezer.

Drinks

• If you've never tried a frozen gin and tonic or vodka and tonic, now's the time. Keep your chosen spirit in the freezer and pour it over ice. It'll be a little thicker than spirits usually are at room temperature. Just add your favourite mixer for a perfectly frosty aperitif.

• Every freezer should have a good supply of ice cubes in it. Did you know that if you use cooled boiled water, instead of water straight from the tap, the ice is less likely to be cloudy? To make your ice cubes prettier and more interesting, you can add slivers of lemon, lime or orange, mint leaves and even edible flowers.

As you can see, I do love an ice cube tray; they're just so incredibly useful when it comes to housing bits and bobs in your freezer! I have six of these in rotation. As soon as the contents of one of them has frozen solid, I pop out the cubes and decant them into freezer bags.

My freezer always contains a few family staples – those everyday items that every household needs and that quite often get gobbled up so quickly that they necessitate an unscheduled dash to the shops. My well-stocked freezer has saved my bacon (sometimes literally) more than once. I always store items such as milk, butter, grated cheese, biscuit dough, bread and tortilla wraps.

More unusually, I keep bags of flour in the freezer when space allows. Why? Well, I do a lot of baking, so I tend to buy flour in bulk, and freezing allows me to store it without it spoiling over time. If you want to do this too, make sure you wrap the paper bag of flour in a plastic freezer bag before freezing as paper is porous – never a good thing in an icy environment. I also freeze individually wrapped sandwich portions so they're ready for grabbing and popping into lunchboxes, where they'll defrost by lunchtime. Simple sandwiches freeze best – buttered bread filled with grated cheese, ham, chicken, beef, peanut butter, etc. Salad items and eggs don't freeze well, and neither does mayonnaise, so leave those out and add a few fresh cucumber batons, cherry tomatoes, raw carrot or celery sticks when packing the lunch. Lastly, I keep

Iceland

To save space in your freezer, flat-freeze sauces, stews and soups in bags (they also defrost much faster) and try to use similar-sized plastic cartons that stack well. Another top tip is to freeze pie fillings in freezer bags lining the pie dish you plan to bake the pie in. Once the filling is frozen, tie the handles and remove it from the pie dish (so you can use that); then when the pie mood takes you, just defrost the block of pie filling directly into the dish, safe in the knowledge that it will fit perfectly.

If space saving is not a priority and in fact you're finding it hard to keep your freezer full, consider freezing some plastic bottles of tap water and using these to fill some of the empty space until you have more interesting items to freeze. A full freezer costs less to run than a half-empty one. Remember, though, that water (in fact, any liquid) expands when frozen, so leave 3cm of 'headspace'. The same applies to stews, soups, curries, anything liquid – also including unopened beer or wine that's been tucked into the freezer for a fast chill; leave it too long and the top will pop off, decorating your freezer with alcohol.

discarded odds and ends of bread in the freezer, bagged up for feeding the ducks.

So what doesn't freeze well? Basically anything with a high water content. Also, don't freeze whole raw eggs (though separated raw yolks and whites freeze like a dream), hard-boiled eggs, lettuce, cucumber, radishes, raw whole or sliced tomatoes (if not in a sauce), low-fat cream cheese, single cream or cottage cheese. Other than that, the freezer's your oyster!

Freezing well requires good storage. I am a bit of a hoarder of things I can keep food in. Old takeaway cartons are a favourite, as are old ice cream tubs (plastic only). These are filled with homemade ready meals, many of which are included in this book. I also love freezer bags in all their guises – the bog-standard basic ones with tie handles and, of course, the wonderful Ziploc® bags. Don't try to freeze food in bags not designed for the freezer; they're simply not thick enough. I've learned the hard way and lost good food to freezer burn (a leathery thick skin as mentioned previously) through using inferior bags.

When it comes to defrosting remember there are so many methods to choose from: overnight in the fridge if you're an organised type; a little faster at room temperature; even faster still using the defrost setting on your microwave; and for some seafood you can simply defrost in cold water. Just make sure you look at the packaging to check what's advised and how long it'll take.

My last word on using and loving your freezer has to be to invest in a freezer pen that's specifically designed for the job – regular ink rubs off in super-cold conditions. Before investing in one, I once defrosted, for the main course of our dinner, some stewed plums. Not exactly the chilli we were all expecting!

Iceland

Pantry Essentials

My freezer is my main store cupboard; I make no apology for it. It's full to the brim with meat, vegetables, homemade meals ready to go and lots of little bits of magic to make meals a little more special; from homemade harissa frozen into ice cube portions to batches of homemade tomato sauce perfect for stirring into pasta or as a base for a curry.

A freezer full of great ideas along with a well-stocked pantry can pretty much always save the day when you're in need. Here are a few of the things I keep close to hand, and if you find after reading this list that your pantry feels a little lacking then please don't set off on your next shopping trip to buy everything on this list. Much better to add a few items each week to spread the cost.

- Black pepper – I get through a lot of freshly ground black pepper so always have a tub ready to fill my pepper grinder back up.

- Biscuits – Yes, I do love to make my own biscuits but I'm also partial to the odd bourbon with a cuppa. Digestives and gingernuts are also great for making cheesecake bases so do keep a couple of packs in.

- Brown sauce – I think you can tell where in the country you're from depending on which sauce you prefer on a bacon sarnie! I love brown sauce with both bacon and sausages but also use it in casseroles, marinades and for dipping scotch eggs into.

- Coconut milk and creamed coconut – Coconut adds such a creamy hint of sweetness, I can't imagine cooking without it. Tins of coconut milk are for more decadent dishes whereas the blocks of creamed coconut are a little easier on the waist line. I simply grate a little into curry sauces as they bubble away.

- Corned beef – Corned beef hash is my guilty pleasure. I always have a tin or two in so that whenever I have an evening alone I can indulge myself. Lots of fried onions, boiled potatoes and corned beef all stirred together and covered in brown sauce. Delicious!

- Chocolate – Oh come on, who doesn't keep a few bars of chocolate in the cupboard? I have milk chocolate for occasional snacking and dark chocolate for baking and enjoying a square with an afternoon coffee.

- Chutney – I'm a chutney fiend, which might well be related to my love of cheese. Chutney, whether tomato, beetroot, onion or mango, brightens up any sandwich, perfect with cheese and biscuits and adds depth to stews, casseroles and marinades.

- Cocoa powder – Don't even think about baking with drinking chocolate. It doesn't work and you won't get the right chocolatey hit. Cocoa is the real deal when it comes to baking. It also makes great hot chocolate and so kills two birds with one stone.

- Crackers – The easiest pudding in the world has to be cheese and biscuits. I always have lots of different cheeses in the fridge and a fair few crackers including oat cakes, water biscuits, cream crackers and more exotic artisan ones with seeds and spices. Crackers are also a good impromptu substitute for bread crumbs.

- Dried herbs – Fresh herbs are, of course, fantastic. However, there's nothing wrong with dried herbs. They're cheaper, have a longer shelf life and still give bags of flavour. I have loads of them and use them liberally.

- Fish – Tinned fish can feel a little reminiscent of school packed lunches. Tuna mayo roll anyone? But it can be fantastic in salads, in fish cakes, to make pâtés, on toast … and fish sauce is very useful to have as a marinade.

- Flour – As a rule I always have plain, self-raising and strong flours ready for any baking urge when it strikes. If you don't bake often or find you don't get through much flour in your cooking then buy small bags and check the use by date. Flour doesn't last forever but you can keep it in the freezer too, see page 14 for details.

- Fruit – I keep dried fruit in for snacking and baking; always sultanas, apricots, dates, prunes, figs, cherries, cranberries and sometimes pineapple and mango too (though these get snaffled rather quickly). Tinned fruit isn't something to be embarrassed about. I often use it to make speedy crumbles on a week night as well as add vitamin C to breakfast in the form of a simple bowl of grapefruit.

- Golden syrup – Liquid gold! Golden syrup is super, super sweet so use it sparingly. It does add a great texture to steamed puddings and is a useful baking ingredient.

- Honey – I always feel a little better about adding honey to a recipe rather than refined sugar. It's just more wholesome. Honey is great stirred into hot water with a squeeze of lemon as a drink for resetting the internal balance. It's also a fine baking substitute for sugar and, of course, tastes great on toast. Don't forget it can add a more subtle sweetness to savoury dishes than pure sugar can.

- Jam – Always strawberry, raspberry, apricot and marmalade. Blueberry is a favourite too. A basic sponge cake is transformed by some fresh cream and a smear of jam. Add fresh fruit to the top and you've really pushed the boat out.

- Lemon juice – I love fresh lemons; it's rare you'll find my fridge bare of them. But bottled lemon juice has a place in my heart too. Sometimes it's just easier to crack open a bottle.

- Marmite® – I'm a lover! It's the savoury hit that some of us crave. I'd eat it by the spoonful straight from the jar, indeed, I have. However, for those less enamoured, it's great for adding depth to gravies and stews.

- Mayonnaise – I will never forget the first time I tried proper homemade mayonnaise; a love affair was born. But it's simply not practical to make mayonnaise on a weekly basis for most of us, so jarred is just fine. I love mayo in sandwiches, as a baked-on topping for chicken (see page 51) and as the base for a dip. You can even bake with it!

- Mustard – I have a few mustards to add heat and flavour to sauces as well as simply serving with meats as a condiment. I love Dijon for its creamy smoothness, English for heat and wholegrain for texture and zing. I was introduced to horseradish mustard recently and admit to having a bit of an addiction to it!

- Noodles – Dried egg noodles are a great fast food when time is short. Just boil, drain and toss in a little oil before stir frying some veg or meat to stir through.

- Oats – Obviously they make great porridge (especially with some maple syrup and frozen red berries thrown in), but are also fantastic for coating homemade fishcakes, adding to crumble toppings or making moreish biscuits.

- Olives – A jar of olives relieved of their brine and topped up with crushed garlic, olive oil and a few sprigs of rosemary can make for a fantastic starter or snack. I have a few jars of green and black olives in the cupboard just in case.

- Olive oil – I keep both bog-standard olive oil and extra virgin in my cupboard. The former for using to cook with and the latter for drizzling over salads.

- Pasta – Oh dear, I seem to collect different shapes of dried pasta. At the time of writing I have fusilli, lasagne, tagliatelle, macaroni, couscous, spaghetti, linguine, minestrone, penne and even some chocolate pasta received as a gift and as yet unused. Different shapes hold sauces better than others. Some are better with meaty sauces, others creamy. Experiment and see what you prefer.

- Peanut butter – I came to peanut butter late, but think I may be making up for lost time. It's fantastic in salad dressings along with coconut milk, a great dipping sauce as satay and, of course, always welcome in sweet treats, especially biscuits.

- Pesto – If you have a jar of pesto, some pasta and a bag of frozen peas, you always have dinner sorted as far as I'm concerned. My kids love pesto stirred through pasta. I do too, as well as pesto spread over bruschetta and also stuffed into chicken breasts.

- Pulses – I keep a good stock of both tinned and dried pulses. I love lentils as well as butterbeans, chickpeas, kidney beans, baked beans and black eyed peas. Dried pulses take a long time to soak and cook, so save time and use a pressure cooker.

- Raising agents – I keep both baking powder (mainly for cakes) and bicarbonate of soda in the pantry. Check the use by dates as both deteriorate in quality over time. Bicarbonate of soda is a great cleaning agent too. I have been known to use it on my teeth and also mixed with a little water as an exfoliator for my skin.

- Rice – I love rice and so do my kids. My favourite has to be fluffy white basmati rice with a little salt and some butter melted over the top. But I also adore risotto, paella and brown rice too. My youngest son has a penchant for rice pudding so you could say we're all big fans of rice, savoury or sweet.

- Salt – I always have regular free flow salt in the cupboard for baking and salting potatoes, rice and the like when cooking, and also sea salt for seasoning food upon serving.

- Soy sauce – Dark and light soy sauce cover all eventualities. We use so much I've taken to buying it in bulk.

- Spices – What can I say? I'm a Leicester girl and was raised on curry. I love my spices! They do deteriorate over time so buy in small quantities and keep an eye on the use by dates.

- Stock cubes – I have a tin full of every stock cube known to man (or woman), as well as some Bouillon powder too. I do make my own stock and keep it in the freezer, but sometimes a stock cube can be just the ticket. Easy and cheap.

- Sugar – I keep a bag of caster sugar for baking, a bag of granulated sugar for drinks and topping pastry puds and a few varying colours of brown sugar for adding a fudgy flavour to crumbles and other baked treats. Icing sugar is useful for making brightly coloured glacé icing for cakes and adding a professional finish to desserts.

- Sweetcorn – Tins of sweetcorn are a useful store cupboard standby for adding colour and sweetness to salsa, mixing into sandwich fillings, making into fritters or simply serving as an easy vegetable with dinner.

- Tinned chopped tomatoes – I get through countless tins of chopped tomatoes, they're just so versatile and impart great flavour whatever the season.

- Tomato ketchup – In sandwiches, in Marie Rose sauce, as a marinade and of course for dipping chips into. Always one on the go in the fridge and one in the cupboard. Well, we could never be without a bottle could we?

- Vegetable oil – I buy a large bottle and use it for any frying where the temperature needs to be really high. Vegetable oil burns at a much higher temperature than olive oil making it perfect for stir and deep frying.

- Vinegar – Malt, white wine, red wine and balsamic are all often used in my kitchen.

- Worcestershire sauce – This is on the same list as Marmite® for me. It adds depth of flavour to sauces, marinades and stews. And is just wonderful splashed over cheese on toast too.

- Yeast – I use dried yeast as well as fresh yeast when baking. Dried yeast is usefully measured out into 7g packets which is the exact amount featured in most recipes. There's nothing quite like the smell and taste of home baked bread, and dried yeast makes baking easier to do off the cuff.

Celebrating 45 Years of Iceland

Iceland began in 1970 with an idea, £30 of start-up capital and a single small shop in Oswestry, Shropshire, selling loose frozen food. We have grown to become one of Britain's best-known brands and the country's number one frozen food specialist, with over 850 stores and 24,000 staff, who have twice voted us the Best Big Company To Work For in the UK. Remarkably, Malcolm Walker, the man who founded Iceland in 1970, is still in charge today.

We floated on the stock market in 1984 and bought our bigger rival Bejam before returning to private ownership in 2005. In the 1980s and 1990s we led the way in removing artificial colours, flavours and non-essential preservatives from our own brand products, along with GM ingredients, and launched the first nationwide home shopping service in the UK.

We have also raised many millions of pounds for good causes through our own Iceland Foods Charitable Foundation, sponsoring fundraising expeditions that have taken the Iceland flag to the top of the world on Mount Everest and to the South Pole.

We pride ourselves on being a convenient and friendly place to do the family's weekly shop, whether that's in store or online, as well as to meet everyone's daily top-up shopping needs.

We are passionate about the 'Power of Frozen', which enables us to deliver an extensive choice of high quality, great-tasting food from fine sources around the world at great value prices.

This book is a celebration of our history, our values and the great food we sell.

Iceland

Chapter 1: Light Bites
Tasty starters, light lunches and gap-filling snacks

Sometimes you don't need much, just a small
plate to ward off hunger. Maybe you have a big
dinner planned for later; perhaps you're just
peckish; or maybe you're searching for a starter
to serve before the main event. It's all here:
small portions, but still big on flavour.

Honey and Mustard Mini Sausages

Honey and mustard sausages are always popular with young and old at any party. So easy to make and so easy to gobble up. I'd recommend making double the quantity you think you might need. These have a way of disappearing fast.

30 cocktail sausages, frozen
3 tablespoons runny honey
3 tablespoons wholegrain mustard
1 tablespoon tomato ketchup
½ teaspoon ground ginger
½ teaspoon freshly ground black pepper
1 sprig of thyme to garnish (optional)

To prepare 5 minutes I **To cook** 30 minutes I
Serves 6 as a snack

• Preheat the oven to 180°C/Fan 160°C/Gas Mark 4 and spread out the sausages in a roasting tray. Roast for 15 minutes until lightly golden, then drain away any fat.

• Mix together all of the other ingredients, pour over the cooked sausages coating them well. Roast for a further 10–15 minutes until sticky. Serve with lots of cocktail sticks.

£ *Save money* . . . by substituting 1½ tablespoons English mustard for the 3 tablespoons (milder) wholegrain mustard. Add an extra tablespoon of tomato ketchup to balance the stronger-flavoured mustard.

✓ *Try* . . . adding some chilli flakes to the marinade for more grown-up guests.

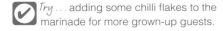

Iceland

Iceland

Asian Chicken Lollipops

This is party finger food at its best: succulent chicken drumsticks marinated in a lightly spiced, sticky Asian marinade. Delicious hot but also cold as picnic fayre the next day.

5 tablespoons soy sauce

2 tablespoons tomato purée

4 garlic cloves, peeled and crushed

1 teaspoon Dijon mustard

2 tablespoons white wine vinegar

1 teaspoon five spice

1 teaspoon ground ginger

8 chicken drumsticks, frozen and
   defrosted or fresh

20g sesame seeds

To prepare 10 minutes plus defrosting and marinating I
To cook 40 minutes I **Serves** 4 as a snack

- Mix all the ingredients together except for the chicken and the sesame seeds and place in a bowl or freezer bag. Using a sharp knife, slash the chicken drumsticks 3 times on each side, cutting about 1cm deep to reveal the flesh. Add the drumsticks, cover the bowl and marinate for at least 2 hours to allow the flavours to develop. If using a bag, tie the top edges to close it and give the contents a little shake.

- Preheat the oven to 180°C/Fan 160°C/Gas Mark 4 and line a roasting tray with foil (this makes less washing up later as this marinade can be tricky to wash off once baked). Place the chicken drumsticks in the tray and bake for 30 minutes.

- Sprinkle the chicken with the sesame seeds and return to the oven for 10 minutes until brown and crisp.

- Check that the chicken is cooked by pushing a skewer into the thickest part of the chicken meat. If the juices run clear, it's done; if not, return the tray to the oven. Eat the chicken drumsticks like lollipops, using the bone as a stick.

Save time ... on the day by planning ahead and marinating the chicken overnight in the fridge.

Save money ... by substituting English mustard for the Dijon mustard and malt vinegar for the white wine vinegar. Just reduce the amounts by half, as these flavours are more pungent.

Try ... reducing the cooking time by 10 minutes and finishing the cooking on the barbecue. Serve with a simple noodle salad.

Iceland

Scallops with Chorizo and Lemon Butter

A starter that tastes as though it took hours of slaving away in the kitchen but is very easy indeed. This recipe scales up or down really well, so it's a perfect treat if you're dining alone; just remember the crusty bread for mopping up the herby chorizo-spiked juices.

50g chorizo, finely chopped
30g salted butter
10ml olive oil
8 scallops, frozen
juice of 1 lemon
20g fresh coriander, finely chopped
    (a small bunch)
1 red chilli, finely chopped

To prepare 5 minutes I **To cook** 8 minutes I **Serves** 4

• Fry the chorizo in the butter and oil for 2 minutes in a large frying pan over a medium heat. Remove the chorizo with a slotted spoon and place in a bowl. Add the frozen scallops to the pan (which will be full of reddish-pink oil from the chorizo).

• Fry the scallops for 3 minutes on each side until cooked through, then return the chorizo to the pan along with the lemon juice, coriander and chilli. Give the pan a good stir. Serve the scallops with crusty bread.

• **NOTE** If you are using defrosted scallops, just sear them for 1 minute on each side.

Save time . . . by swapping the fresh chilli for frozen chilli and avoid some of the chopping.

Save money . . . by using 50ml bottled lemon juice instead of fresh lemon and leaving out the chilli and coriander.

Iceland

Iceland

Garlic Butter Tiger Prawns

These tiger prawns are a super-speedy starter, even quicker to cook than to prepare. They feature the classic combination of garlic, butter and parsley and are served with thick crusty rolls for mopping up the juices. A great introductory recipe for cooks who are a little daunted by tiger prawns!

20 raw tiger prawns, frozen and
   defrosted or fresh
20g salted butter
20ml olive oil
4 garlic cloves, peeled and crushed
1 lemon, zested and juiced
6 stalks of fresh parsley, finely chopped

To prepare 25 minutes plus defrosting I **To cook** 5 minutes I **Serves** 4–5 as a starter

• Make sure the prawns are thoroughly defrosted. Before cooking decide whether you are leaving the heads on or removing them. To take the heads off, simply hold each head between your thumb and forefinger, holding the body of the prawn in your other hand, and snap the head backwards. It should come off easily.

• Heat the butter and olive oil in a large frying pan over a medium heat until the butter has melted. Then add the garlic and prawns and pan-fry for 3 minutes. Add the lemon zest and juice. Stir well and fry for another minute until the prawns are pink. Remove from the heat and stir in the fresh parsley. Serve with lots of warm crusty bread.

(£) *Save money* ... by substituting tiger prawns with king prawns and using dried parsley instead of fresh; just use 1 teaspoon.

(✓) *Try* ... ringing the changes by using a lime instead of a lemon and coriander instead of parsley. Add a finely chopped fresh red chilli just before serving and you've got a fiery version of this classic.

Iceland

Winter Vegetable Soup
with Herby Croutons

This is the ultimate comfort food. A thick, wholesome soup seasoned with salt, pepper and a little lemon juice to really bring out the earthy root vegetable flavours. The herby baked croutons make this hearty soup really special.

For the soup

6 tablespoons olive oil
1 onion, peeled and roughly chopped
1 teaspoon salt
2 carrots, peeled and roughly chopped
1 stick celery, including leaves, roughly
    chopped
1 leek, trimmed at top and bottom, sliced
    and rinsed
1 parsnip, peeled, trimmed at top and
    bottom and roughly chopped
¼ swede, peeled and roughly chopped
1 potato, peeled and roughly chopped
1 teaspoon freshly ground black pepper
1 stock cube
juice of 1 lemon

For the croutons and to garnish

3 or 4 sprigs of fresh parsley, finely
    chopped
2 thick slices of bread

Save time … avoid all of the peeling and chopping by using frozen vegetables.

Save money … by using 50ml bottled lemon juice instead of fresh and omitting the herbs.

Try … grilling some bacon until really crisp and crumbling it over the soup just before serving. Or stir a teaspoon of pesto into the soup just before serving.

To prepare 30 minutes I **To cook** 15 minutes I **Serves** 4–6

• Prepare all the vegetables, making sure the pieces are all roughly the same size – about 2–3cm is ideal.

• Heat 2 tablespoons of the oil in a large saucepan over a medium heat. Place the onions in the pan along with the salt and sweat them for 5 minutes, then add the carrots and celery. Leave these vegetables to sweat for 10 minutes, stirring occasionally.

• Add the leek, parsnip, swede, potato and black pepper, and stir well.

• Make up 1.5 litres of stock using boiling water and the stock cube, then add this to the pan. Cover and leave to simmer for 15 minutes, until a knife will pass through all the vegetables easily. In the meantime preheat the oven to 200°C/Fan 180°C/ Gas Mark 6 for the croutons.

• Place half of the parsley in a large bowl with the remaining 4 tablespoons of olive oil. Cut the bread into good-sized cubes, about 2cm square, and stir into the herby oil. Line a baking tray with non-stick baking paper and bake the croutons for 10–12 minutes until crunchy and browned.

• Add the lemon juice to the soup and use a stick blender or regular blender to blitz the soup to a smooth consistency. How much you blend it is up to personal taste. If you don't have a blender, use a potato masher or push the soup through a colander. Gently reheat the soup before serving if necessary.

• Ladle the soup into bowls, add a sprinkle of the reserved parsley and garnish with the croutons.

Iceland

Iceland

Baked Scotch Eggs

For those who don't fancy deep frying – whether because of calories or safety – these are the perfect alternative. Oven-baked Scotch eggs still have bags of flavour from herby sausage meat and well-seasoned breadcrumbs. They're best served with good old-fashioned brown sauce.

5 large eggs

270g sausage meat or 5 good quality sausages, removed from their casing, frozen and defrosted or fresh

1 tablespoon finely chopped fresh thyme

1 tablespoon finely chopped fresh parsley

½ teaspoon freshly ground black pepper

45g fresh breadcrumbs

45g plain flour, seasoned with a little salt and pepper

2 tablespoons olive oil

To prepare 50 minutes plus defrosting I **To cook** 25 minutes I **Serves** 4

- Place 4 of the eggs in a pan of cold water, place on the hob and bring to the boil without a lid. Once the water is boiling, pop the lid on, remove from the heat and set the timer for 7 minutes. Remove the eggs and place in cold water, still in the shells. Once they are cool enough to handle, peel them, remembering that they are soft boiled and so relatively fragile.

- Mix the sausage meat with the herbs until well combined. Divide the meat into quarters and place each quarter on a piece of cling film about 25cm square. Put another piece of cling film on top and squash the meat into a circle roughly 10cm in diameter and about 3mm thick. Remove the top piece of cling film, place an egg in the centre and pull the bottom piece of cling film up around the sides, encasing the egg in sausage meat. Use your hands (over the cling film) to mould the meat around each egg. Chill the eggs, still in the cling film, for 15 minutes.

- Preheat the oven to 200°C/Fan 180°C/Gas Mark 6. Line a baking tray with non-stick baking paper.

- Beat the remaining egg and stir the pepper into the breadcrumbs. Set up a 'dipping station' with one bowl for the seasoned flour, one for the beaten egg and one for the seasoned breadcrumbs. Remove the eggs from the cling film and coat each with flour, then egg, then breadcrumbs. Place on the baking tray, drizzle with oil and bake for 25 minutes until golden brown. Serve warm or cold, as you prefer.

£ *Save money* ... by using dried herbs instead of fresh ones – just 1 teaspoon of each. Or use falafel to encase the eggs for a more economical, vegetarian version.

✓ *Try* ... adding 50g finely chopped chorizo to the sausage meat along with 1 teaspoon paprika. Or try replacing one-quarter of the sausage meat with black pudding.

Garlic Mushrooms
with Blue Cheese Dip

Who doesn't love the classic pub starter of breaded garlic mushrooms? Here's how to make them at home – plus a tasty blue cheese dip that marries perfectly with the buttery, juicy, garlicky mushrooms.

For the mushrooms

3 garlic cloves, peeled and crushed

60g salted butter

12 medium-sized mushrooms (about 300g)

45g plain flour, seasoned with a little salt and pepper

1 large egg, beaten

70g breadcrumbs, frozen or fresh

For the dip

50g natural or Greek yoghurt

35g mayonnaise

60g Danish blue cheese, crumbled

1 tablespoon lemon juice (fresh or bottled)

¼ teaspoon salt

½ teaspoon freshly ground black pepper

To prepare 20 minutes I **To cook** 15 minutes I **Serves** 4 as a starter

- Preheat the oven to 180°C/Fan 160°C/Gas Mark 4. Line a large baking tray with non-stick baking paper.

- Heat the garlic and butter together in a large saucepan on the hob, over a low heat, until the butter has melted and is just starting to bubble. Add the mushrooms and stir gently for 5 minutes. Remove from the heat and set aside.

- Place the flour in a bowl, the beaten egg in a small mug or cup (it's easier to immerse the mushrooms completely in a mug than in a bowl) and the breadcrumbs in another bowl. Using a fork, spear each mushroom, then dip it in the flour first, ensuring that it is well covered, then in the egg and lastly in the breadcrumbs. Carefully use a knife to remove the mushroom from the fork and place on the baking tray. Repeat until all the mushrooms are coated. Bake for about 15 minutes until golden.

- In the meantime, make the blue cheese dip. Combine all the ingredients and blitz either with a stick blender or in a food processor; for a chunkier dip, mash with a fork. Serve the warm garlic mushrooms with a pot of the cold dip on the side.

- **NOTE** There will be a little garlic butter left over from the mushrooms – just perfect for brushing on slices of part-baked baguette before baking.

£ *Save money* . . . by substituting a few spoonfuls of mayonnaise spiked with paprika for the blue cheese dip.

✓ *Try* . . . using any leftover blue cheese dip the next day as a relish in sandwiches. It's also great with chicken salad on sourdough bread.

Iceland

Iceland

Baked Bhaji Bites

A less calorific, but equally tasty version of the classic onion bhaji. These are perfect as a snack, in lunchboxes and even on a picnic. Larger versions would make a great alternative to veggie burgers.

For the bhajis
5 tablespoons vegetable oil, plus extra
    for drizzling
450g onions, peeled and finely sliced
    (about 6 medium onions)
½ teaspoon salt
½ teaspoon ground cumin
½ teaspoon turmeric
1 teaspoon garam masala
½ teaspoon cayenne pepper
2 teaspoons tomato purée
90g plain flour

For the cucumber raita
3 tablespoons natural yoghurt
1 tablespoon grated cucumber
a pinch of dried mint
a little salt and pepper

To prepare 30 minutes | **To cook** 15 minutes | **Makes** 12

- Preheat the oven to 180°C/Fan 160°C/Gas Mark 4 and line a baking tray with non-stick baking paper. Heat the oil in a large frying pan over a medium heat and fry the onions for about 10 minutes until soft, but not brown. Add the salt, cumin, turmeric, garam masala and cayenne pepper, stir, and then fry for 2 minutes. Remove from the heat.

- Mix the tomato purée with 2 tablespoons of cold water and stir into the onion mixture along with the flour. Stir until the onions are well coated, then, using a spoon or your fingers, drop 12 mounds of the mixture on to the baking tray, placing them about 5cm apart. Drizzle each with a teaspoon of oil and bake for 12–15 minutes until sizzling and golden brown.

- While the bhajis are baking, make the raita. Simply combine all the ingredients in a small bowl. Serve alongside the bhajis.

Try ... using red onions instead of white ones for extra sweetness. You can even substitute grated carrot for half of the onion if you like.

Cheddar and Marmite® Scones

These very cheesy scones have a tang of Marmite®, and are even better with some leftover ham thrown in. Great for lunchboxes or served warm with a cooked breakfast. If you're a Marmite® addict, slather them with butter and yet more Marmite®!

1 tablespoon Marmite®
145ml very cold whole or semi-skimmed
  milk, plus extra for brushing
300g plain flour, plus extra for dusting
15g baking powder
1 teaspoon freshly ground black pepper
90g very cold salted butter, cut into
  1cm cubes
90g strong Cheddar, grated

To prepare 30 minutes plus chilling | **To cook** 15 minutes | **Makes** 5–6

• Using a fork, whisk the Marmite® into the milk for a few minutes; set aside. Mix the flour, baking powder and black pepper together in a large bowl until well combined. Add the butter and stir with a blunt knife until all the pieces are well coated, then rub in with your thumbs and forefingers until you have a breadcrumb-like consistency. Next, add 60g of the grated cheese and gently stir.

• Pour the Marmite®-milk over the butter and flour mixture, being careful to scrape in any Marmite® that hasn't quite dissolved, and bring the dough together with a blunt knife. Use your hands to squeeze the mixture together, then wrap the dough in cling film and chill for 30 minutes.

• Preheat the oven to 220°C/Fan 200°C/Gas Mark 7 and check that the rack is near the top of the oven. Cover a baking sheet with non-stick baking paper.

• Place the dough on a lightly floured work surface and roll to about a 3cm thickness. Cut out 5 or 6 scones using a 6cm scone cutter dipped in flour and cutting straight down, without twisting or turning. Place the scones on the baking sheet, about 5cm apart (you can re-work the leftover dough, if you like, to make extra scones, but these will not be as tender as the first ones). Brush the tops of the scones with a little milk, making sure that none of it runs down the sides as this will stop a good rise; then sprinkle with the remaining cheese. Bake immediately for 15 minutes until the tops are golden brown, the cheese is bubbling and the scones are well risen.

• **NOTE** If you aren't a lover of Marmite® you can just leave it out altogether!

Save time ... by using ready grated Cheddar.

Try ... experimenting by adding different ingredients. How about half a red onion, finely chopped, or a handful of sliced olives or some chives?

Iceland

Iceland

Chapter 2: Easy Mid-Week Suppers
For busy week nights, when time is short

Busy days working and organising the family
can leave you short of time and inspiration when
it comes to dinnertime. These ideas are all low
on stress and preparation time but high on
taste, and economical to boot.

Chilli Con Carne Enchiladas

This is such a satisfying mid-week meal – a quick beef chilli simmered until tender, used to fill soft flour wraps, then baked with a cheesy sauce until crunchy and golden and served with a simple homemade guacamole.

For the enchiladas

2 tablespoons vegetable oil

1 onion, peeled and finely chopped, or use frozen diced onions

2 garlic cloves, peeled and crushed

300g minced beef, frozen or fresh

1 x 400g can of chopped tomatoes

2 tablespoons tomato purée

1 teaspoon chilli powder

1 teaspoon ground cumin

1 teaspoon ground cinnamon

1 teaspoon freshly ground black pepper

2 squares dark chocolate, grated (about 30g)

1 x 400g can of red kidney beans, drained

4 tortilla wraps

150g soured cream

150g crème fraîche

150g strong cheese such as Cheddar, grated

For the guacamole

1 avocado, stoned, peeled and mashed

½ red onion, finely chopped

1 tomato, finely chopped

juice of 1 lime

a little fresh coriander, chopped (optional)

To prepare 35 minutes | **To cook** 30 minutes | **Serves** 4

- You will need 2 rectangular ovenproof dishes, each about 30 x 15cm.

- Preheat the oven to 180°C/Fan 160°C/Gas Mark 4. Grease the ovenproof dishes with 1 tablespoon of the oil (for both). Heat the remaining oil in a large frying pan over a medium heat. Fry the onion until it starts to brown slightly, then add the garlic and minced beef. Stir fry for about 5 minutes until browned. Add the chopped tomatoes, tomato purée, chilli, cumin, cinnamon and black pepper, and give the pan a stir. Fill the empty tomato can half full with cold water and add that too. Simmer to reduce the chilli for 20 minutes, adding the grated chocolate just before the end.

- Stir in the red kidney beans, remove from the heat and spoon a quarter of the mixture into the centre of each tortilla. Wrap the tortilla up like a cigar, leaving both ends open, and place 2 in each dish, with the 'join' underneath. Mix the soured cream and crème fraîche with two-thirds of the cheese and spread this over the top of the enchiladas. Sprinkle with the remaining cheese and bake for 30 minutes.

- To make the guacamole, just mash all the ingredients together using a fork.

- Serve the enchiladas with the guacamole, a green salad or simply on their own.

Save time ... by using a jar or packet mix of chilli sauce instead of making your own and using ready grated Cheddar.

Try ... adding some fresh chilli to ramp up the heat. Or make this lower in fat by using Quorn™ mince.

Iceland

Iceland

Ginger and Garlic Pork Stir Fry

Sometimes the simplest combination of flavours can be the most moreish. Soy, garlic and ginger, mixed together with a little honey, is an easy marinade to whip together quickly, and it works equally well with pork or chicken.

2 tablespoons dark soy sauce
3 garlic cloves, peeled and crushed
1 teaspoon ground ginger
2 teaspoons runny honey
330g pork loin steaks, trimmed of fat and
    cut into strips (about 4 or 5 loin steaks),
    frozen and defrosted or fresh
185g frozen broccoli
2 tablespoons vegetable oil
1 red pepper, deseeded and cut into
    strips
8 spring onions, roots removed and
    sliced into approximately 2cm chunks

To prepare 20 minutes plus defrosting I **To cook** 15 minutes I
Serves 4

- Make the marinade by stirring together the soy sauce, garlic, ginger and honey in a bowl, or pour into a freezer bag. Add the pork strips and leave to marinate in the fridge for 10 minutes.

- Boil the broccoli florets for 5 minutes, then drain.

- Heat the oil in a wok or large frying pan over a very high heat. Once it's sizzling hot, add the pork and marinade. Move the pork around the wok/pan and after 2 minutes add the pepper strips, broccoli and spring onions, in that order, stirring after each addition. Keep stir frying, moving the pork and vegetables around the pan for another 5 minutes.

- Serve the pork with steamed rice or noodles.

Save time ... by using frozen Oriental vegetable mix.

Try ... some different vegetables, such as pak choi, shiitake mushrooms and Chinese cabbage, and throw some toasted cashew nuts over the finished dish.

Iceland

Rosemary and Garlic Lamb Meatballs

These meatballs are heaven. Sticky fried onions lend a sweetness that pairs perfectly with rosemary and garlic. They're good with a homemade tomato sauce served over pasta, rice or quinoa or in a pitta pocket with lots of salad.

For the tomato sauce

1 x 400g can of chopped tomatoes
200ml cold water
1 tablespoon tomato ketchup
1 tablespoon tomato purée
1 carrot, peeled and finely chopped
1 stick celery, finely chopped
1 teaspoon black pepper
a pinch of salt

For the meatballs

2 tablespoons olive oil, plus extra for
   greasing the roasting tray
1 teaspoon salt
1 teaspoon sugar
1 onion, peeled and finely chopped, or
   use frozen diced onions
450g lamb mince, frozen and defrosted
   or fresh
50g breadcrumbs
3 tablespoons water
4 garlic cloves, peeled and crushed
1 tablespoon very finely chopped fresh
   rosemary
1 teaspoon freshly ground black pepper

To prepare 25 minutes plus defrosting | **To cook** 30 minutes, including the tomato sauce | **Serves** 4

- If you want to make your own tomato sauce to serve with the meatballs, get this on the stove first. Place all the ingredients in a saucepan over a very low heat and simmer for 30 minutes, stirring occasionally. If you want a smoother sauce, you can blitz it with a stick blender or in a liquidiser.

- Preheat the oven to 180°C/Fan 160°C/Gas Mark 4 and grease a roasting tray with a drizzle of olive oil.

- Pour the olive oil into a frying pan along with the salt and sugar; add the chopped onions and fry over a low heat for 10 minutes until they are browned and slightly sticky. Remove from the heat and allow to cool a little.

- Use your hands to mix together the defrosted lamb, sticky onions, breadcrumbs, water, garlic, rosemary and black pepper. Press the mixture down into the bowl and score into quarters using a knife. Make 4 meatballs out of each quarter of the mince, each about the size of a golf ball. Place the 16 meatballs in the roasting tray, not touching, and bake for 15–20 minutes until browned and sizzling.

- Serve them over rice, pasta or quinoa with the tomato sauce ladled over the top.

Try . . . making burgers out of the same mixture and popping them on the barbecue. Roll the mixture into 4 balls, then flatten each into a burger shape. Serve in burger buns with minty coleslaw on the side; just stir a tablespoon of finely chopped fresh mint through some ready-prepared coleslaw.

Iceland

Iceland

Parmesan-Crusted Chicken

Who knew that a simple jar of mayonnaise could transform chicken breasts from an often somewhat unimaginative dinner into something succulent and flavoursome? This recipe is just a template – try whatever herbs and cheese you prefer, though I've found that keeping a quarter of the cheese as Parmesan or Grana Padano bolsters the cheesy flavour.

4 chicken breast fillets, frozen
150g mayonnaise
1 garlic clove, peeled and crushed
60g Parmesan cheese, grated
1 teaspoon English mustard
1 tablespoon thyme leaves
½ teaspoon freshly ground black pepper

To prepare 10 minutes I **To cook** 50 minutes I **Serves** 4

• Preheat the oven to 200°C/Fan 180°C/Gas Mark 6 and line a roasting tray with non-stick baking paper. Place the chicken breasts on the tray and cook from frozen for 25 minutes.

• Mix together the rest of the ingredients, except for 20g of the cheese. Remove the chicken from the oven and divide the mixture equally between the chicken breasts, carefully smoothing it over the top with a spoon, then sprinkle with the remaining cheese. Roast for a further 25 minutes until cooked through.

• Serve with roast potatoes and carrots.

• **NOTE** If you're using fresh chicken, just divide the mixture between the uncooked chicken breasts and roast at 180°C/Fan 160°C/Gas Mark 4 for 25–30 minutes until cooked through.

£ *Save money* ... by swapping Parmesan for slightly cheaper, yet still tasty, Grana Padano cheese. You can also use 1 teaspoon of dried thyme rather than fresh herbs.

✓ *Try* ... slicing the chicken and serving it on a bed of watercress, cucumber ribbons and steamed new potatoes. Drizzle with your favourite salad dressing.

Iceland

Cowboy's Sausage Casserole

*A proper one-pot, hearty dinner with no need for sides.
This is exactly the kind of food we all crave as the autumn
nights draw in. We especially like to eat it on Bonfire
Night before watching the fireworks.*

2 tablespoons olive oil

12 sausages, frozen

1 onion, peeled and finely chopped, or
use frozen diced onions

1 carrot, peeled and chopped into 1cm
cubes

2 garlic cloves, peeled and crushed

4 small potatoes, peeled and cut into
3cm chunks

2 x 400g cans of chopped tomatoes

2 tablespoons tomato purée

1 teaspoon Marmite®

1 teaspoon sugar

1 teaspoon salt

1 teaspoon freshly ground black pepper

2 sprigs of thyme, leaves only

1 bay leaf

2 x 400g cans of butter beans, drained
and rinsed

To prepare 25 minutes | **To cook** 45 minutes | **Serves** 4

• Heat the oil in a large saucepan (a stock pot is ideal if you
have one) and fry the sausages and onions on a medium heat
for about 10 minutes until browned.

• Add the rest of the ingredients, apart from the butter beans,
turn the heat to low and simmer for 35 minutes, with the lid on,
stirring occasionally.

• Add the butter beans and simmer for a further 10 minutes.

• Serve the casserole either on its own or with some warm
crusty bread.

Save time ... let your slow cooker do the
hard work while you're out; first brown
the sausages in a frying pan, then add all the
ingredients to the slow cooker and leave it on
low for 2 hours.

Save money ... by using ½ teaspoon dried
thyme instead of the fresh herbs. You
can also substitute baked beans for the butter
beans, so long as you rinse them first to wash
away the sweet tomato sauce.

Iceland

Iceland

Spaghetti Carbonara

This tasty fast food is ready quicker than a takeaway can be delivered. I serve mine with lots of black pepper, extra grated cheese and a side of garlic bread.

1 teaspoon salt
300g dried spaghetti
1 tablespoon olive oil
200g bacon lardons
1 garlic clove, peeled and crushed
2 large eggs, beaten
90g Grana Padano cheese, grated
1 teaspoon freshly ground black pepper

To prepare 5 minutes | **To cook** 15 minutes | **Serves** 4

• Pour boiled water from the kettle into a large saucepan, add the salt and bring back to the boil. Add the spaghetti and simmer for 10 minutes (or according to the packet instructions). Just before draining, remove ¼ mug of the pasta water and save.

• While the spaghetti is cooking, heat the oil in a large frying pan, add the lardons and fry them over a medium heat until browned. Reduce the heat, add the garlic and stir fry for 1 minute, then add the drained spaghetti, along with the saved pasta water (this helps to separate the strands and will thin the sauce a little). Stir well and remove from the heat.

• Stir half the cheese into the beaten eggs, add to the pasta and immediately stir really well, lifting the spaghetti up with two spoons to ensure that the eggs do not curdle (the residual heat from the pasta and frying pan will cook the eggs).

• Serve the spaghetti with lots of freshly ground black pepper and sprinkle with the rest of the cheese.

• **NOTE** Do not serve lightly cooked eggs to babies, pregnant women, the elderly or anyone with a weak immune system.

£ *Save money* ... by substituting Cheddar for the Grana Padano and streaky bacon or even ham (which needs no cooking) for the lardons. Admittedly it won't be as authentic, but it will still be delicious.

✓ *Try* ... adding frozen peas to the pasta just before the end of cooking for a vitamin C boost. Or fry some mushrooms with the lardons for a more earthy flavour and add shredded cooked chicken to the sauce too.

Iceland

Iceland

Prawn and Pea Curry

A curry that tastes this fresh and vibrant shouldn't be so quick to make. Serve it with lots of fluffy basmati rice, chopped fresh coriander or a simple naan for scooping up the delicious sauce.

4 tablespoons vegetable oil

1 large onion, peeled and finely chopped, or use frozen diced onions

1 teaspoon salt

1 teaspoon freshly ground black pepper

1 tablespoon sugar

3 garlic cloves, peeled and crushed

800g fresh tomatoes (about 9 medium), finely chopped

2 tablespoons tomato purée

1 teaspoon garam masala

1 teaspoon chilli powder

325g cooked and peeled large prawns, frozen and defrosted

200g frozen petits pois

coriander to garnish (optional)

To prepare 15 minutes plus defrosting | **To cook** 30 minutes | **Serves** 4

• Heat 2 tablespoons of the vegetable oil in a saucepan and fry the onion for 5 minutes over a medium heat until starting to soften. Turn the heat to low, add the salt, pepper, sugar and garlic, and fry for another 5 minutes. Add the tomatoes and tomato purée and simmer for 20 minutes, then remove from the heat.

• Once the tomato sauce is ready, heat the remaining two tablespoons of vegetable oil in a frying pan over a medium heat, add the garam masala and chilli powder, and stir fry for 1 minute. Stir in the tomato sauce, prawns and peas, and simmer for 5 minutes until the peas are heated through.

£ *Save money* ... by swapping the fresh tomatoes for 2 x 400g cans of chopped tomatoes. You can also reduce the amount of prawns by half and add more peas.

✓ *Try* ... playing with the heat. This is a medium-hot curry but it can be toned down by using less chilli powder or made super-hot with lots of fresh chilli. If you overdo the heat, cool the sauce a little with a swirl of fresh natural yoghurt before serving, or serve the curry with a cucumber raita (see page 39).

Mediterranean Fish Stew

A hearty and honest fish and potato stew spiked with garlic, parsley and a little lemon juice. Once the seafood's defrosted it's on the table in just over half an hour, but tastes as though you've been in the kitchen all day.

400g cooked, premium seafood selection (contains mussels, squid and king prawns), frozen and defrosted

3 tablespoons olive oil

1 onion, peeled and chopped into roughly 1cm chunks, or use frozen diced onions

100ml dry white wine

1 red pepper, deseeded and cut into strips

400g potatoes, peeled and chopped into 4cm cubes

1 x 400g can of chopped tomatoes

a pinch of sugar

1 vegetable stock cube

1 teaspoon freshly ground black pepper

juice of 1 lemon

2 tablespoons finely chopped flat-leaf parsley

To prepare 20 minutes plus defrosting | **To cook** 25 minutes | **Serves** 4

- Heat the oil in a large saucepan on a very low heat and fry the onion for 8–10 minutes until soft but not browned. Add the garlic and stir fry for a further 2 minutes.

- Turn up the heat and add the wine, pepper strips, potatoes, canned tomatoes, sugar, 500ml vegetable stock made using the stock cube and boiling water, plus the black pepper. Leave to simmer uncovered for 15–20 minutes until the potatoes are tender and a knife will pass through them easily.

- Turn the heat down, add the defrosted cooked seafood (and any juices), stir and let simmer for 3 minutes until warmed through.

- Add the lemon juice and parsley, check for seasoning and add a little salt if you wish (though the stock cube should provide some), and stir well.

- Ladle into bowls. Serve with crusty bread for mopping up all the juices.

(£) *Save money* ... by leaving out the wine and simply adding a little more stock and using white fish fillets instead of seafood. You can also swap the fresh lemon juice for 50ml of bottled lemon juice and the fresh parsley for 1 teaspoon dried parsley.

(✓) *Try* ... adding whole black tiger prawns to turn this into a really luxurious, impressive dish.

Iceland

Iceland

Pesto and Lemon Baked Salmon

A simple fish supper made extra-special with a crunchy, lemony breadcrumb pesto crust. Best of all, you can prepare the crunchy crumb topping ahead of time.

4 salmon fillets, frozen
80g green pesto
zest of 2 lemons
60g fresh breadcrumbs
½ teaspoon black pepper

To prepare 10 minutes | **To cook** 30 minutes | **Serves** 4

• Preheat the oven to 220°C/Fan 200°C/Gas Mark 7. Place the frozen salmon fillets on a baking sheet lined with non-stick baking paper and bake in the oven.

• In the meantime mix together the rest of the ingredients. After the salmon has been in the oven for 10 minutes, divide the mixture into quarters and spread carefully over the top of each salmon fillet. Bake for a further 20 minutes until cooked through.

• Serve the salmon with roasted Mediterranean style vegetables or simply new potatoes dressed in butter and lemon juice (from the zested lemons).

• **NOTE** You can make this recipe with fresh salmon fillets by reducing the cooking time to 15–20 minutes and spreading the salmon with the pesto mixture before baking at 200°C/Fan 180°C/Gas Mark 6.

Try ... grating Grana Padano cheese over the top of the salmon once it's baked and sprinkling with toasted pine nuts to serve.

Quorn™ and Lentil Cottage Pie with Crunchy Potato Topping

This is a cottage pie with a difference. It's one for vegetarians – with Quorn™ mince and lentils replacing beef – but it is guaranteed to please meat eaters too. Crunchy diced potatoes, flavoured with fresh thyme, are a speedy alternative to the usual mash.

3 tablespoons olive oil

1 onion, peeled and finely chopped, or use frozen diced onions

1 carrot, peeled and diced

1 celery stick, including leaves, finely chopped

300g Quorn™ mince, frozen

1 teaspoon freshly ground black pepper

2 tablespoons fresh thyme leaves

1 x 400g can of chopped tomatoes

2 tablespoons tomato purée

1 teaspoon Marmite®

50g dried red lentils

1 vegetable stock cube

750g potatoes, peeled and diced into 2cm cubes (about 8 medium potatoes)

To prepare 15 minutes I **To cook** 55 minutes I **Serves** 4

- Heat 1 tablespoon of the oil in a large saucepan and sweat the onion, carrot and celery for 5 minutes over a medium heat until soft. Add the mince, fry for 2 minutes, then add the black pepper, 1 tablespoon of the fresh thyme, tomatoes, tomato purée, Marmite®, lentils and stock, made from adding the stock cube to 500ml boiling water.

- Turn the hob down to low and leave to simmer, uncovered, for 30 minutes. Preheat the oven to 200°C/Fan 180°C/Gas Mark 6. Parboil the potatoes for 5 minutes, drain and toss them in the remaining oil and thyme.

- Pour the Quorn™ and lentil mixture into a casserole dish about 27 x 20 x 5cm and arrange the potatoes on top. Bake for 25 minutes until the potatoes are golden and a knife will pass through them easily.

Save time ... you could replace this thyme-flavoured potato topping with frozen crispy potatoes.

Save money ... by using 2 teaspoons of dried thyme instead of fresh.

Try ... adding a can of drained mixed beans to provide further texture and protein and replacing the topping with sweet potato mash.

Iceland

Chapter 3: Comfort Classics
Traditional and modern favourites

Sometimes it's one of those days when you need
a bowl of something comforting – both physically
restorative and mentally soothing, the kind of
food that takes us back to childhood, reminding us
of a simpler time. This chapter is food for the soul.

Steak and Stout Pie

This warming pie is great with a puff pastry lid,
but equally good as a hearty stew.

3 tablespoons plain flour, plus a little
   extra for rolling
1 teaspoon salt
1 teaspoon freshly ground black pepper
800g diced beef, frozen or fresh
3 tablespoons olive oil
2 onions, peeled and finely chopped, or
   use frozen diced onions
200g mushrooms, halved
500ml stout
1 beef stock cube
4 sprigs of thyme, leaves only
500g all-butter puff pastry
egg wash (1 egg beaten with a pinch
   of salt)

To prepare 30 minutes I **To cook** 2 hours 50 minutes I
Serves 4–6

• Preheat the oven to 160°C/Fan 140°C/Gas Mark 3. Mix the flour,
salt and pepper in a bowl and toss the beef in it. Heat the oil in a
large frying pan on a medium heat and fry the beef in batches of
8–10, turning the pieces to brown them. Don't overcrowd the pan
or the beef will steam rather than brown. Place the browned beef
in a large lidded casserole dish approximately 27 x 20 x 5cm.

• Fry the onions and mushrooms for 5 minutes in the frying pan
with the remaining oil (you may need to add a little extra). Add the
stout, stock cube (crumbled) and thyme leaves, and bring to a
simmer. After 5 more minutes transfer the mixture to the casserole
dish, cover with the lid (or tightly fitted foil if you don't have one)
and place in the oven for 2 hours.

• After 2 hours, check the beef is tender and falling apart easily,
remove from the oven and leave to cool. When completely cool
(you can leave it overnight in the fridge), pour the filling into a pie
dish about 20 x 4cm and preheat the oven to 200°C/Fan 180°C/
Gas Mark 6. Using a lightly floured rolling pin on a floured work
surface, roll the pastry to measure about 3cm larger than the pie
dish and to the thickness of a £1 coin.

• Trim the edges of the pastry to remove some strips about 2cm
wide. Use a pastry brush to brush the rim of the pie dish with egg
wash and fix the strips of pastry to the dish, pressing down firmly.
Brush the pastry-lined dish rim with egg wash, then place the
rolled-out pastry lid over the top, being careful not to stretch the
pastry too much or it will shrink when baking. Press down gently
around the edges and use scissors to cut the edge of the pastry to
about 5mm larger than the rim of the dish.

• Press the prongs of a fork around the pastry rim, then use a sharp
knife to cut a cross shape 4cm in each direction in the centre of
the pie. Brush the pie with egg wash and bake for 40–50 minutes
until golden brown, well risen and bubbling. Serve with honey
roasted carrots and buttery mash.

£ *Save money* . . . by letting your slow
cooker do the actual cooking; the
steak and stout filling will take 3½ hours on
the low setting. Also try substituting 1
teaspoon of dried thyme for the fresh thyme
and use beef stock with a dash of
Worcestershire sauce in place of the stout.

✓ *Try* . . . adding raw parsnip to the filling
before baking to add extra flavour.

Iceland

Iceland

Easy Cottage Pie

This is a hands-off cottage pie. Instead of using mashed potatoes, we're just slicing the potatoes really thinly and using foil or a casserole lid to create steam to cook them. The prep time can be as little as 20 minutes if you work fast. Then just sit and relax while the house fills with comfort food aromas.

For the filling

2 tablespoons olive oil

1 onion, peeled and finely chopped, or use frozen diced onions

1 carrot, peeled and diced

1 stick celery, including leaves, finely chopped

3 tablespoons plain flour

500g beef mince, frozen or fresh

1 beef stock cube

1 tablespoon fresh thyme leaves

1 tablespoon tomato purée

1 tablespoon Worcestershire sauce

½ teaspoon freshly ground black pepper

For the potato topping

800g potatoes, unpeeled and very thinly sliced (about 2mm) (about 3 large potatoes)

¼ teaspoon salt

¼ teaspoon freshly ground black pepper

2 tablespoons olive oil

To prepare 35 minutes I **To cook** 1 hour I **Serves** 4–6

- Preheat the oven to 200°C/Fan 180°C/Gas Mark 6. Fill and boil the kettle.

- Heat the oil in a large frying pan on a medium heat for 1 minute. Add the onion, carrot and celery and soften for 2 minutes, stirring occasionally. Stir the flour into the mince, coating it evenly. Add to the pan and brown for 5 minutes, stirring occasionally.

- Make up 400ml stock with boiling water from the kettle and the stock cube. Add the thyme, tomato purée, Worcestershire sauce and black pepper to the stock. Stir to mix and pour into the frying pan. Simmer for 10–15 minutes, allowing the sauce to thicken a little.

- Meanwhile toss the sliced potatoes in the salt, pepper and oil.

- Pour the cottage pie filling into a large casserole dish about 27 x 20 x 5cm. Cover the top with the sliced potato; you should have enough for about 3 layers. Cover with a tightly fitting lid/foil and bake in the oven for about 1 hour, removing the lid/foil for the last 20 minutes.

- Serve with buttered peas or green beans.

Save time ... by using frozen crispy potato slices; just add to the top and cook as above.

Save money ... by using 1 teaspoon of dried thyme instead of fresh.

Try ... adding some soaked dried porcini mushrooms to the pie mixture for extra depth of flavour. You could also try frozen mash.

Iceland

Sweet and Sour Pork

A takeaway classic that's incredibly easy to make at home.
I serve this with fluffy rice or sometimes stir-fried noodles.
You can make this with chicken or Quorn™ too if you prefer.

700g diced pork, frozen and defrosted
  or fresh
3 tablespoons malt vinegar
1 teaspoon salt
2 tablespoons vegetable oil
1 tablespoon light soy sauce
1 tablespoon cornflour
3 tablespoons tomato ketchup
2 tablespoons sugar
1 teaspoon Worcestershire sauce
1 x 435g can of pineapple pieces in juice
3 garlic cloves, peeled and crushed
1 onion, peeled and thinly sliced
1 red pepper, deseeded and chopped
  into 2cm pieces

To prepare 15 minutes plus defrosting I **To cook** 20 minutes I
Serves 4

• Place the pork in a bowl with 1 tablespoon of the vinegar and
the salt. Stir well and leave for 5 minutes to marinate. Heat the
oil in a large frying pan or wok over a high heat, then add the
pork (including the marinade) and fry until lightly browned and
cooked through.

• In the meantime, make the sauce by mixing together the
remaining vinegar with the soy sauce, cornflour, tomato
ketchup, sugar, Worcestershire sauce and 80ml of the
pineapple juice.

• Remove the pork from the pan or wok with a slotted spoon and
set aside, leaving the juices in the pan. Add the garlic, fry for
1 minute, then add the onion and peppers. Fry for 3 minutes.
Lastly return the pork to the pan and add the pineapple chunks
(but not the rest of the pineapple juice – you can discard this
or drink it) and the sauce. Stir well and simmer for 2–4 minutes
until the sauce has thickened.

• **NOTE** If you're using frozen pork, simply defrost and cut into
3cm chunks.

Save time . . . by making the sauce
ahead of time and keeping it in the
fridge. You can also use frozen Oriental
vegetable mix to avoid having to chop the
vegetables.

Try . . . swapping the onions for spring
onions, adding a little heat with a
tablespoon of fresh, finely chopped ginger
and serving with a handful of cashew nuts
thrown in.

Iceland

Iceland

Chicken, Cider and Bacon One-Pot

A simple one-pot supper of juicy chicken thighs, smoky bacon, onions, mustard and cider. This is so easy and wholesome; even better, there's no need to prepare any extra vegetables unless you want to, as they're already included.

3 tablespoons olive oil

4 chicken thighs, skin on, bone in, frozen

2 onions, peeled and sliced, or use frozen diced onions

200g smoked bacon, diced (about 7 rashers)

2 tablespoons Dijon mustard

400ml cider

2 tablespoons roughly chopped fresh parsley

200g petits pois, frozen

2 tablespoons natural yoghurt

1 tablespoon cornflour

To prepare 25 minutes | **To cook** 70 minutes | **Serves** 4

- Heat the oil in a large saucepan or stock pot over a medium heat. Place the chicken thighs in the pan, skin side down, to brown, then turn over.

- Add the onions and bacon, stir and leave to fry for 5 minutes. Add the mustard, cider and parsley, and bring to the boil.

- Reduce the heat to a simmer and leave to cook with the lid on for 60 minutes until the chicken thighs are cooked through and the juices run clear.

- Add the peas and yoghurt, stir well and simmer gently for a further 5 minutes.

- Remove 3 tablespoons of the sauce and mix with the cornflour; pour this back into the pan, stir and heat for 5 more minutes.

- Serve with boiled potatoes, rice or quinoa, or simply on its own with crusty bread to mop up the juices.

- **NOTE** If you're using fresh chicken thighs simply reduce the simmer time to 40 minutes.

Save time ... try using scissors to cut the parsley; it's quicker and less messy than using a knife and chopping board.

Save money ... by using chicken stock instead of cider if you prefer; just add a sliced and cored eating apple too.

Try ... swapping the parsley for tarragon. It has a slight aniseed flavour that works really well with chicken.

Iceland

Oven-Baked Rosemary Leg of Lamb

This is perfect for a late and lazy Sunday lunch – you just throw everything into the roasting tray and forget about it. The meat juices mingle with the roasted carrots and swede to create a base for a fantastic gravy.

For the lamb

2 carrots, peeled and sliced in half lengthways
2 onions, peeled and sliced in half
½ swede, peeled and cut into large chunks
2 tablespoons vegetable oil
1 leg of lamb (about 2kg), frozen
2 rosemary sprigs, leaves only, finely chopped
1 teaspoon salt
2 teaspoons freshly ground black pepper
1 lamb or vegetable stock cube

For the gravy

meat juices from the lamb
2 tablespoons plain flour
65ml red wine
a little gravy browning (optional)

To prepare 20 minutes I **To cook** 3 hours 50 minutes I **Serves** 4–6

- Preheat the oven to 200°C/Fan 180°C/Gas Mark 6. Arrange a large length of foil under your roasting tray; it should be long enough to wrap around the whole tray twice later on. Place the carrots, onions and swede in the bottom of the tray.

- Heat the oil in a large frying pan. Holding the lamb with a clean tea towel, carefully brown it on as many sides as you can get into contact with the heat. Place the lamb on the vegetables in the tray.

- Mix together the rosemary, salt and pepper and rub into the top of the lamb. Make up 500ml stock using the stock cube and boiling water, then pour into the base of the roasting tray (not over the top of the lamb or it will wash off the herbs and seasoning).

- Use the foil to wrap the whole tray until it's well sealed and place in the oven. This is the hardest part of the recipe as if you don't take the time to do it well, the lamb won't be cooked. The steam needs to stay inside the foil parcel. Don't keep opening the oven door during the cooking time, as it will lose too much heat.

- After 3 hours remove the tray from the oven, remove the foil and then return to the oven for 50 minutes, while you make gravy and finish any last touches to side dishes.

- To make the gravy, tip 3 tablespoons of the meat juices into a saucepan and heat on the hob until starting to sizzle. Add the flour and whisk vigorously until smooth. Add the wine and more of the meat and vegetable juices gradually, whisking all the time, until you have reached the thickness of gravy you prefer. Simmer for 4 minutes, then add a little gravy browning if you like your gravy to have a darker hue.

✓ *Try* … adding some extra flavour with garlic. Cut 3 or 4 garlic cloves into thin slices, cut little slits all over the lamb and insert the garlic slices in these.

Iceland

Iceland

Slow-Cooked Beef Ragù

A deep, rich ragù slow-cooked in the oven until the beef is falling apart. Perfect for serving over pasta or with rice.

3 tablespoons olive oil

1 teaspoon salt

1 teaspoon freshly ground black pepper

800g diced beef, frozen or fresh

2 sticks celery, leaves included, finely chopped

2 carrots, peeled and finely chopped

2 onions, peeled and finely chopped, or use frozen diced onions

2 garlic cloves, peeled and crushed

220g streaky bacon, finely chopped (about 7 rashers)

1 tablespoon finely chopped fresh rosemary

1 tablespoon fresh thyme leaves, plus extra to garnish

2 tablespoons tomato purée

200ml red wine

1 x 400g can of chopped tomatoes

1 beef stock cube

To prepare 30 minutes I **To cook** 3 hours I **Serves** 4

- Preheat the oven to 160°C/Fan 140°C/Gas Mark 3 and find a large casserole dish approximately 27 x 20 x 10cm with a tightly fitting lid.

- Heat the oil in a frying pan over a medium heat, stir the salt and pepper into the beef and fry in batches of 8–10 pieces until brown, being careful not to overcrowd the pan, otherwise the beef will steam rather than brown. Once browned, transfer the beef to the casserole dish with a slotted spoon.

- Fry the celery, carrots, onions, garlic and bacon for 10 minutes in the remaining beef fat, stirring well. Add the herbs and tomato purée, fry for a further 2 minutes, then add the wine and turn the heat to high. Simmer for 5 more minutes, then tip the mixture into the casserole dish. Return the pan to the heat, pour in the chopped tomatoes and 600ml stock made using boiling water and the beef stock cube. Stir well and pour into the casserole dish.

- Place the lid (or very tightly fitted foil) on the casserole dish and place in the oven for 3 hours until the beef is very tender and falling apart.

- Serve with pasta or rice.

£ *Save money* . . . by letting your slow cooker do the actual cooking; the ragù will take 5 hours on the low setting. Also try substituting 1 teaspoon each of dried herbs for the fresh ones and more stock for the red wine.

✓ *Try* . . . swapping the rosemary and thyme for oregano, for a more Mediterranean-style ragù.

Macaroni Cheese
with Crunchy Bacon Topping

Macaroni cheese the traditional way with a very cheesy roux sauce made even better by sprinkling with crunchy bacon.

350g dried macaroni

30g salted butter

40g plain flour

500ml milk

½ teaspoon English mustard

½ teaspoon salt

1 teaspoon freshly ground black pepper

¼ teaspoon freshly grated nutmeg

250g mature Cheddar, grated

60g Gruyère, grated

125g drained mozzarella, chopped into approximately 2cm chunks

300g smoked bacon (about 10 rashers)

2 tablespoons olive oil

To prepare 25 minutes I **To cook** 20 minutes I **Serves** 4

• Preheat the oven to 160°C/Fan 140°C/Gas Mark 3. In a saucepan of boiling water, cook the pasta for 10–12 minutes or according to the packet instructions until al dente. Drain, rinse in cold water and set aside.

• Meanwhile, make the cheese sauce. Melt the butter in a large saucepan over a low heat. Add the flour and whisk for 1 minute until it forms a ball. Add the milk, little by little, whisking well as you go, then turn the heat up to medium. Continue to whisk for 2–5 minutes until the sauce thickens. Add the mustard, salt, pepper, nutmeg, Cheddar and Gruyère, stir and remove from the heat. Stir in the pasta and pour into a casserole dish about 27 x 20 x 5cm. Sprinkle the mozzarella on the top and bake for 20 minutes.

• While the macaroni is baking, fry the bacon in the oil until really crisp. Dry it on kitchen paper, then finely chop and sprinkle over the macaroni cheese 5 minutes before removing from the oven.

• Serve with salad or green vegetables.

Save time ... by using ready grated cheese and skipping the bacon topping. Instead, try adding a handful of breadcrumbs to the top, halfway through the cooking time, for some crunch and texture.

Save money ... by leaving out the Gruyère and mozzarella. This recipe is also great for using up any odds and ends of cheese in the fridge. Just grate and chuck them in!

Try ... studding the top with cherry tomatoes to add bursts of sweetness.

Iceland

Fish and Chip Pie

All the favourites in one pie: a layer of bright mushy peas, simple white fish in a soothing white sauce and a layer of crisp, cheesy homemade oven-baked chips.

6 white fish fillets (about 840g), frozen
   and defrosted
2 x 300g cans of mushy peas
600g potatoes, washed and cut into
   1.5cm-thick chip-shaped batons
   (about 6 medium potatoes)
30g salted butter
25g plain flour
320ml milk
¾ teaspoon salt
1 teaspoon freshly ground black pepper
2 tablespoons olive oil
65g mature Cheddar, grated

To prepare 25 minutes plus defrosting I **To cook** 30 minutes I **Serves** 4

• Ensure that the fish is fully defrosted and drained of any juices before you begin (you can squeeze the fish to do this). Preheat the oven to 190°C/Fan 170°C/Gas Mark 5. Cut each fillet into 4 equal-sized pieces. Open the mushy peas and spoon them into a large, deep, casserole dish approximately 27 x 20 x 10cm. Parboil the potato batons until you can just slip a knife into them, then drain and set aside.

• Make the white sauce. Melt the butter in a medium–sized saucepan over a low heat. Once it's melted, add the flour and whisk until completely smooth. Add the milk, little by little, whisking well as you go, then turn the heat up to medium. Continue to whisk gently as the milk heats; once the sauce is thick and bubbling, remove from the heat. Add ¼ teaspoon salt, ½ teaspoon pepper and the fish strips, stir well and pour the sauce over the peas.

• Tip the drained potato batons over the pie, drizzle with a little olive oil and sprinkle the remaining salt and pepper on top. Bake for 20–25 minutes until golden. Just before serving add the grated cheese and grill for a couple of minutes until golden brown and crisp.

• Don't forget to put a bottle of malt vinegar on the table; this is fish and chip pie, after all!

Save time ... by using fish in parsley sauce and frozen cheesy potato slices as the topping.

Try ... adding freshly chopped mint to the peas and some prawns to the white sauce. Serve with some sliced pickled onions for the full chippy supper effect.

Double Cheese, Onion and Potato Pie

So simple but so tasty: fresh spring onions and caramelised white onion stirred through milky, cheesy mashed potato, with extra cheese in the shortcrust pastry, then baked until golden brown and tender.

For the pastry

140g cold butter, cut into 1cm cubes
280g plain flour, plus extra for dusting
50g Grana Padano or other hard cheese, finely grated
100ml very cold water

For the filling

700g potatoes, peeled and sliced thinly
1 tablespoon olive oil
½ teaspoon sugar
1 large onion, peeled and finely chopped, or use frozen diced onions
40ml milk, plus a little extra for fixing and glazing the pastry
385g mature Cheddar, grated
½ teaspoon English mustard
1 teaspoon salt
1 teaspoon freshly ground black pepper
5 spring onions, green tops trimmed slightly, thinly sliced

Save time . . . by using frozen mashed potato and a 500g block of ready-made shortcrust pastry.

Try . . . making this really special by swapping the milk for double cream and throwing in 2 tablespoons of chopped fresh flat-leaf parsley, along with a chopped leek softened in butter. Experiment with the cheese, too. How about using some Gruyère and a little Stilton?

To prepare 30 minutes plus chilling | **To cook** 30 minutes | **Serves** 4–6

- First make the pastry. Rub the butter into the flour until you have a fine breadcrumb consistency. Stir through the grated Grana Padano and add the water, stirring with a blunt knife until the dough starts to come together. Scoop into a ball, flatten, wrap in cling film and chill for 30 minutes.

- In the meantime prepare the filling. Boil the potatoes in a large pan of water until tender. Drain them well and transfer back into the saucepan. Heat the olive oil in a frying pan over a low heat, add the sugar and chopped onion (not the spring onions), and fry for about 10 minutes until brown and caramelised. Remove from the heat.

- Mash the potatoes until smooth, then add the milk, Cheddar, mustard, salt and pepper, and mash again until well combined. Lastly, stir through the caramelised onions and the spring onions. Spoon the potato filling into a mound in a pie dish approximately 20 x 15 x 7cm.

- Preheat the oven to 200°C/Fan 180°C/Gas Mark 6. Using a floured rolling pin on a lightly floured work surface, roll out the chilled pastry just larger than the pie dish and about the thickness of a £1 coin. Use a pastry brush dipped in a little milk to brush around the edges of the pie dish.

- Slide both hands, palm side up and fingers spread, under the pastry and gently lay it over the pie. Press the pastry around the rim of the pie dish, then trim it using a sharp knife. Use the prongs of a fork to press the edges down. Use a pastry brush to brush the surface of the pie with a little milk (or egg beaten with a pinch of salt if you prefer) and bake for 25–30 minutes.

- Serve with carrots and green beans or peas.

Iceland

Iceland

Chapter 4: Food to Impress
Special suppers perfect for entertaining

Sometimes you want to pull out all the stops. It might be a big celebratory meal for all the family; maybe you're having friends over for a posh dinner; perhaps it's date night; or it could just have been one of those weeks – time to give yourself a well-deserved special treat. If you need a recipe to impress, then you've come to the right chapter.

Ostrich Fillet
with Peppercorn Sauce

*Ostrich is a very lean meat which has a strong flavour
and hence needs to be paired with equally robust flavours.
So in steps this traditional, creamy, peppercorn sauce.*

4 ostrich fillets, frozen and defrosted
2 tablespoons olive oil
1 large onion, peeled and finely
   chopped, or use frozen diced onions
2 tablespoons green peppercorns
2 tablespoons pink peppercorns
½ teaspoon salt
150ml white wine (preferably dry)
1 beef stock cube
90ml double cream

To prepare 5 minutes plus defrosting I **To cook** 25 minutes I
Serves 4

• Fry the ostrich fillet in 1 tablespoon of the olive oil, to your
taste; between 2 and 5 minutes on each side, according to
how rare you like your meat. Place on a plate to rest, covered
in foil and a clean tea towel. Leave the meat juices in the pan.

• To make the sauce, first add the rest of the oil to the juices in
the pan and warm over a medium heat. Fry the onion in this for
about 5 minutes until soft, then add the peppercorns and salt.
Turn the heat up to high, add the wine and 400ml beef stock,
made using the beef stock cube and boiling water, and let the
sauce simmer and reduce for 5–10 minutes until about half of
the liquid remains.

• Put the ostrich fillets back into the pan, reduce the heat to low
and stir in the cream, ensuring that it doesn't boil.

• Serve immediately with chips or boiled and buttered Jersey
Royals (if they're in season), along with grilled portobello
mushrooms or green beans.

Save time . . . by making the sauce the
night before, up until the cream stage.
Simply keep it covered in the fridge.

Try . . . serving this classic sauce over
beef fillets, using red wine instead of
white and perhaps throwing in some sliced
mushrooms also. You can also make this
slightly lower in fat by substituting reduced-fat
crème fraîche for the double cream.

Iceland

Iceland

Beef Goulash

Beef goulash seems to be popular with all the family; it's pleasingly sweet from the vegetables, with beef that falls apart on your fork and a sauce that's just mildly spiced...

3 tablespoons olive oil

800g diced beef, frozen or fresh

2 tablespoons plain flour

2 tablespoons paprika

1 teaspoon salt

1 teaspoon freshly ground black pepper

2 onions, peeled and finely chopped, or use frozen diced onions

2 garlic cloves, peeled and crushed

2 tablespoons tomato purée

1 x 400g can of chopped tomatoes

1 beef stock cube

2 red peppers, deseeded and finely sliced

To prepare 30 minutes I **To cook** 2 hours 30 minutes I **Serves** 4

• Preheat the oven to 160°C/Fan 140°C/Gas Mark 3 and find a large casserole dish approximately 27 x 20 x 10cm with a tightly fitting lid.

• Heat the oil in a frying pan over a medium heat, stir the beef into the flour, paprika, salt and pepper, and fry in batches of 8–10 pieces until brown, being careful not to overcrowd the pan, otherwise the beef will steam rather than fry. Once browned, transfer the beef to the casserole dish with a slotted spoon.

• Fry the onions and garlic for 10 minutes in the remaining beef fat, stirring well. Add the tomato purée, fry for 1 more minute, then add the chopped tomatoes and turn the heat to high. Simmer for 5 more minutes, then tip into the casserole dish. Add 600ml stock made using boiling water and the beef stock cube.

• Place the lid (or very tightly fitted foil) on the casserole dish and place in the oven for 1½ hours. Remove from the oven, add the peppers, replace the lid and cook for another hour.

• Serve with pitta bread, boiled potatoes or rice.

 Save time ... by using frozen quick cook peppers.

 Try ... letting your slow cooker do the actual cooking; the goulash will take 5 hours on the low setting.

Iceland

Moroccan Lamb
with Paprika Dumplings

This delicately spiced lamb stew is not only finished with dried apricots and almonds but also topped with feather-light, fluffy paprika and coriander dumplings. Guaranteed to impress!

For the stew

3 tablespoons olive oil

800g lamb chump, cut into 3cm pieces, frozen and defrosted or fresh

4 onions, peeled and sliced

1 teaspoon ground ginger

1 teaspoon ground cumin

1 teaspoon ground coriander

1 teaspoon ground cinnamon

1 teaspoon paprika

½ teaspoon salt

1 teaspoon freshly ground black pepper

2 garlic cloves, peeled and crushed

2 tablespoons tomato purée

1 lamb stock cube

160g dried apricots, cut in half (about 25)

40g flaked almonds

4 tablespoons finely chopped fresh coriander

For the dumplings

240g self-raising flour

2 teaspoons baking powder

½ teaspoon salt

1 teaspoon paprika

180ml milk

30g salted butter, melted

1 tablespoon finely chopped fresh coriander

£ *Save money* . . . by letting your slow cooker do the actual cooking; the lamb will take 4 hours on the low setting. You could also leave out the fresh coriander and the flaked almonds.

To prepare 35 minutes plus defrosting I **To cook** 2 hours I **Serves** 4

• Preheat the oven to 160°C/Fan 140°C/Gas Mark 3. Heat the oil in a large frying pan over a medium heat and fry the lamb in batches of 8–10 pieces until browned, being careful not to overcrowd the pan otherwise the lamb will steam rather than fry. Remove the lamb with a slotted spoon and place in a casserole dish with a tightly fitting lid, approximately 27 x 20 x 10cm.

• Fry the onions, ginger, cumin, ground coriander, cinnamon, paprika, salt and pepper in the lamb fat for 2 minutes, then add the garlic, tomato purée and lamb stock made with 600ml boiling water and the lamb stock cube. Turn up the heat and bring to a simmer, then pour into the casserole dish. Fit the lid and cook in the oven for 2 hours.

• Half an hour before the end of the cooking time, add the apricots to the stew and make the dumplings. Sieve together the flour, baking powder, salt and paprika into a bowl. Stir well. In a jug stir the milk, melted butter and coriander together. Pour the milk into the flour and stir with a blunt knife. Once the ingredients are combined (don't over-mix!), drop 10 heaped tablespoons on top of the stew with a 2cm space between them, cover with the tightly fitting lid and continue baking for 15 minutes. Check that the dumplings are cooked through by spearing with a knife; it shouldn't be sticky. If they need a little longer, replace the lid and bake for another 5 minutes (the main reason they may not have baked is an ill-fitting lid; the dumplings require steam to be cooked through).

• Just before serving, lightly toast the almonds in a dry frying pan. Stir them as they toast and carefully watch them, as they can burn in seconds. Once browned, tip them into a bowl (or they will carry on browning in the pan's residual heat), then scatter over individual portions along with the fresh coriander.

Iceland

Iceland

Cajun Pulled Pork with Spicy Beetroot, Apple and Carrot Slaw

This is real soul food that's great for a gathering or simply for a relaxed Sunday lunch. You can easily double, triple or quadruple this recipe for a crowd. If there are any leftovers, keep them in the fridge and treat someone to a really special packed lunch.

For the pork

2 onions, peeled and sliced
1 teaspoon ground chilli
1 teaspoon paprika
1 teaspoon ground cumin
1 tablespoon brown sugar
1 tablespoon finely chopped fresh thyme
2 teaspoons wholegrain mustard
1 teaspoon salt
1 teaspoon freshly ground black pepper
4 garlic cloves, peeled and crushed
3 tablespoons tomato ketchup
800g pork shoulder joint, frozen
150ml white wine vinegar
150ml cider

For the slaw

1 carrot, peeled
1 fresh beetroot, uncooked, peeled
1 apple, peeled and cored
½ red chilli, finely chopped
1 tablespoon lemon juice
65g crème fraîche
¼ teaspoon salt
½ teaspoon freshly ground black pepper

To prepare 30 minutes I **To cook** 2 hours I **Serves** 4

• Preheat the oven to 160°C/Fan 140°C/Gas Mark 3. Place the onions in a large casserole dish with a tightly fitting lid.

• Make the Cajun rub. In a small bowl combine the chilli, paprika, cumin, sugar, thyme, mustard, salt, pepper, garlic and ketchup. Stir well and rub all over the pork shoulder, then place the joint on top of the onions.

• Pour the vinegar and cider around the shoulder, cover with the lid (or very tightly fitting foil if you don't have a lid) and roast for 2 hours. The pork should easily come apart with two forks after this time and is therefore ready to serve (don't throw away the onions! They'll be really spicy and soft – perfect as a hot-style chutney).

• Just before you serve, make the slaw. Grate the carrot, beetroot and apple and mix them with the chilli, lemon juice and crème fraîche. Season with salt and pepper, then serve alongside the pulled pork with soft rolls.

• **NOTE** The pork will cook in the same amount of time whether frozen or fresh.

£ *Save money* ... (and time) by making the pulled pork in a slow cooker. Simply leave it on low for 4½ hours.

✓ *Try* ... doubling the chilli in the slaw if you prefer a little more heat in your food. This Cajun pulled pork is also a real treat when used as a relish on top of a burger at a barbecue.

Iceland

Wild Boar and Apple Sausage, Squash and Sage Tray Bake

A sausage tray bake is welcome comfort food any day of the week but here we're taking it to the next level with wild boar and apple sausages.

12 wild boar and apple sausages, frozen and defrosted
3 tablespoons olive oil
1 butternut squash
2 onions, peeled and halved
4 large potatoes, peeled and cut into 3cm chunks
1 teaspoon dried sage
½ teaspoon salt
1 teaspoon freshly ground black pepper

To prepare 20 minutes plus defrosting I **To cook** 45 minutes I **Serves** 4–6

• Preheat the oven to 190°C/Fan 170°C/Gas Mark 5. Place the sausages in a large roasting tray and drizzle with the olive oil.

• Prepare the squash by peeling it, cutting in half lengthways, removing the seeds and then cutting each half widthways into slices about 2cm thick. Add these to the roasting tray along with the onions and potatoes. Sprinkle with sage, salt and pepper, and stir well. Roast for 40–45 minutes until the vegetables are tender and the sausages golden brown.

• Serve on its own or with onion gravy.

Save time ... by just giving the potatoes a quick scrub before quartering them, rather than peeling them.

Iceland

Iceland

Jerk Chicken

I'm not pretending for a second that this is authentic jerk chicken but it's pretty close, combining chilli-hot crisp skin with juicy chicken flesh.

½ teaspoon ground allspice

1 tablespoon freshly ground black pepper

½ teaspoon ground cinnamon

½ teaspoon ground nutmeg

½ teaspoon ground cloves

1 tablespoon fresh thyme leaves

6 spring onions including green parts, finely chopped

2 green chillies, finely chopped

2 tablespoons dark brown sugar

1 teaspoon salt

60ml dark soy sauce

30ml malt vinegar

8 chicken thighs, skin on, frozen and defrosted or fresh

To prepare 20 minutes plus defrosting and marinating I
To cook 25 minutes I **Serves** 4

• Marinate the chicken for at least 6 hours before you plan to barbecue or oven-bake it, but overnight is better if you have the time. Ensure the chicken is thoroughly defrosted before you begin. Simply combine all the ingredients (apart from the chicken thighs) and mix well. I often use a mini food processor for this to ensure that I don't get any chilli on my skin. Pour the marinade into a freezer bag, add the chicken thighs, seal and leave to chill in the fridge.

• Grill on the barbecue until the juices run clear when you pierce the thickest part of the thigh. The exact time depends on the thickness of the thighs, but you should chargrill them in the middle of the barbecue for a few minutes on each side, then move them to the edge and leave for around 25 minutes.

• If the weather is miserable, or if you don't have a barbecue, you can bake the chicken in an oven preheated to 180°C/Fan 160°C/Gas Mark 4 for about 25 minutes until the juices run clear when you pierce the thickest part of the chicken thigh. The larger the chicken thighs, the longer they will take to cook.

• Serve with coleslaw, corn on the cob, plain white rice or the traditional rice and peas.

Save time ... by marinating the chicken for just an hour or two. It won't be quite as strong in flavour but will still be spicy. You could also try using a ready-mixed jerk seasoning too.

Save money ... by substituting 1 teaspoon of dried thyme for the fresh thyme.

Iceland

Scallop, Salmon and Dill Pie

Fish pie is always a winner, but when it's made with scallops and salmon you know you're looking at a different class of pie. Add a creamy white wine and dill sauce, top it with mashed potato, bake until golden and you have a really special, yet easy-to-make dinner.

For the topping

900g potatoes, peeled and cut into 3cm chunks (about 8 medium)
40g salted butter, cubed
65ml milk
1 teaspoon freshly ground black pepper

For the filling

3 tablespoons olive oil
500g salmon, cut into 3cm cubes, frozen
500g scallops, frozen
2 tablespoons flour
210ml dry white wine
1 tablespoon finely chopped fresh dill
125g crème fraîche
½ teaspoon salt
1 teaspoon freshly ground black pepper

To prepare 30 minutes I **To cook** 7 minutes I **Serves** 4

• Boil the potatoes until tender, drain well, mash and stir in the butter, milk and pepper.

• In the meantime, make the filling. Pan-fry the frozen salmon fillets for 6 minutes on each side until cooked through, then break up and place in a casserole dish measuring approximately 27 x 20 x 5cm.

• Add the scallops to the pan and fry for 3 minutes on each side. Transfer to the casserole dish. Add the flour to the pan juices and stir with a whisk. Add the white wine, stir well and turn up the heat. The sauce will thicken a little after 2–4 minutes of continuous stirring (stay with it!).

• Stir in the dill, crème fraîche, salt and pepper, then tip the salmon, scallops and any juices back into the pan. Heat through, pour back into the casserole dish and top with the mashed potato. Heat the grill and place the pie under it for 5–7 minutes until the top is browned and crunchy.

• Serve with buttered peas, green beans or salad.

• **NOTE** If you are using fresh salmon fillets fry for 2 minutes on each side, then break up in the casserole dish as above. If you are using defrosted scallops, reduce the frying time to 1 minute on each side.

✔ *Try* . . . adding some king prawns to the filling to make it even more special. You could also make this pie in individual pie dishes and top them with a little grated Parmesan for serving at a dinner party.

Iceland

Iceland

Italian Sea Bass Parcels

A ridiculously easy and nutritious dinner that tastes sumptuous. The sea bass is baked in a foil parcel so it steams in its own juices and keeps all the flavour. Perfect served with couscous, new potatoes or a crisp green salad.

4 sea bass fillets, frozen
4 tablespoons olive oil
2 lemons
4 garlic cloves, peeled and crushed
4 tablespoons finely chopped fresh parsley
4 tablespoons finely chopped fresh basil
32 cherry tomatoes, on the vine if possible

To prepare 5 minutes I **To cook** 25 minutes I **Serves** 4

• Preheat the oven to 200°C/Fan 180°C/Gas Mark 6. Cut 4 pieces of foil, 4cm longer than the fish fillets and triple the width. Place a fillet in the centre of each piece of foil, and on top of each drizzle 1 tablespoon olive oil, the juice of half a lemon, 1 garlic clove, ½ tablespoon parsley, ½ tablespoon basil and 8 cherry tomatoes. Seal the parcels by folding the foil over and scrunching it tight, leaving some air above the fish to allow it to steam.

• Bake in the oven for 25 minutes until the fish is cooked through. Cooking times may vary according to how thick the fillets are; the thicker the fillet, the longer the baking time.

• Serve the fish sprinkled with the remaining parsley and basil.

✓ *Try* ... adding different flavourings. How about lime and sweet chilli, or thinly sliced ginger with soy and garlic or lemon and coriander? You could even put out all the ingredients on the kitchen table and let everyone choose their own flavourings before you bake.

Iceland

Lobster Gratin

Lobster is such a deliciously rich tasting seafood that can be tricky to prepare. Here we use lobster tails to get masses of flavour from the meat without all the faff of preparing a whole lobster. This parsley and breadcrumb topped cheesy gratin is the perfect way to give lobster the extra special treatment it deserves.

200g lobster tails, frozen and defrosted
30g salted butter
1 onion, peeled and finely chopped, or use frozen diced onions
1 teaspoon salt
2 tablespoons plain flour
2 teaspoons freshly ground black pepper
100ml white wine (preferably dry)
juice of 1 lemon
2 teaspoons Dijon mustard
2 garlic cloves, peeled and crushed
240ml milk
100g Grana Padano cheese, grated
4 tablespoons finely chopped fresh parsley
30g fresh breadcrumbs

To prepare 10 minutes plus defrosting I **To cook** 5 minutes I **Serves** 2

• Defrost the lobster tails at room temperature for about 3.5 hours or overnight in the fridge.

• Remove the lobster tails from all packaging and cut the lobster down the back with a sharp pair of scissors. Crack open the shell and remove the meat. Cut into pieces about 2cm in size.

• Melt the butter in a saucepan over a medium heat. Add the chopped onion and salt and soften for 10 minutes. Add the lobster meat and stir.

• Preheat the grill, then add the flour and pepper to the onions and stir well with a wooden spoon until well blended. Add the wine, lemon juice, mustard and garlic, stirring all the time as it bubbles. Then add the milk, turn up the heat and continue to stir until the sauce thickens; it will look curdled to begin with, but keep stirring and it will come together. Add half the cheese, stir and pour into a baking dish measuring approximately 27 x 20 x 5cm (or use small individual dishes)

• Lastly top with the parsley, breadcrumbs and the rest of the cheese. Grill for about 5 minutes until browned.

• Serve the lobster with a green salad and some crusty bread for mopping up the juices.

Try ... serving this with blanched asparagus chopped into the sauce and with a tall glass of chilled prosecco.

Iceland

Iceland

Paella

A little reminder of summer holidays past: an authentic chicken, chorizo and mixed seafood paella with bags of colour and flavour. If you close your eyes, you're almost back in Spain.

a pinch of saffron

2 tablespoons finely chopped flat-leaf parsley

1 chicken stock cube

3 tablespoons olive oil

100g chorizo, diced into 1cm pieces

1 onion, peeled and finely chopped

1 yellow pepper, deseeded and chopped into 1cm pieces

3 garlic cloves, peeled and crushed

1 teaspoon turmeric

½ teaspoon paprika

300g paella rice

100g peas, frozen

1 chicken breast, cut into thin strips, frozen and defrosted or fresh

400g cooked, premium seafood selection (contains mussels, squid and king prawns), frozen and defrosted

juice of 1 lemon

250ml dry white wine

12 tiger prawns, frozen and defrosted

To prepare 25 minutes plus defrosting I **To cook** 20–25 minutes I **Serves** 4

- Fill a jug with 750ml boiling water, and the saffron, parsley and stock cube. Leave to infuse.

- Heat the oil in a really large frying pan or wok (otherwise the stock will spill over the sides later) over a medium heat. Fry the chorizo for 3–5 minutes until it's crisp at the edges and has released its red oil. Add the onion, pepper, garlic, turmeric and paprika and fry for 5 minutes, stirring regularly. Add the rice, stir well until it's all coated and fry for 2 minutes, then add the stock mixture. Stir well and leave to simmer for 15 minutes, stirring occasionally.

- After 15 minutes add the peas, raw chicken pieces, seafood selection, lemon juice and white wine. Stir well, ensuring that all the chicken pieces are well covered. Place the tiger prawns on the top and turn the heat up slightly. If you're using raw prawns, remember that they're ready when they're completely pink all over. Otherwise simmer for a further 5–7 minutes until all the liquid has been absorbed, then serve.

Save time ... by using frozen ready diced onions, frozen quick cook sliced mixed peppers and cooked sliced chicken. Simply add the chicken right at the end to heat through for 2 minutes.

Save money ... by leaving out the saffron or adding more stock instead of the wine.

Try ... adding 30ml sherry along with the white wine. Also, you can easily make this paella vegetarian by adding lots more peppers, onions, peas and even chickpeas to the rice instead of the seafood, chorizo and chicken.

Iceland

Chapter 5: Sweet Treats
Tempting puddings and bakes

Now and again we all yearn for something
sweet – a little treat to enjoy after supper or
with a cuppa in the afternoon, be it a brownie,
a slice of lemon tart, a bowl of apple pie with
custard or a slice of cheesecake.

Apple Pancakes

These fluffy American-style pancakes are studded with chunks of fresh apples and laced with cinnamon. They are as delicious for dessert as they are for a weekend breakfast treat.

For the apples

3 apples, peeled, cored and cut into
    1cm chunks
1 tablespoon lemon juice
½ teaspoon ground cinnamon

For the pancakes

180ml milk
30ml lemon juice
130g plain flour
25g caster sugar
1 teaspoon baking powder
½ teaspoon bicarbonate of soda
½ teaspoon salt
½ teaspoon ground cinnamon
1 large egg
40g butter, melted
vegetable oil

To prepare 15 minutes **To cook** 10–20 minutes
Makes 10–12 pancakes

- Place the apples, lemon juice and cinnamon in a small saucepan and cook over a low heat for about 10 minutes until the apples are soft. Set aside.

- Make the pancake batter. Mix the milk and lemon juice in a jug and set aside. In a bowl, stir the flour, sugar, baking powder, bicarbonate of soda, salt and cinnamon together.

- Crack the egg into the jug with the milk and lemon in it and add the butter. Whisk, then pour this liquid over the dry ingredients. Use a fork to mix the ingredients until they are just combined, then stir in half the apples. Don't over-whisk or the pancakes will be tough.

- Heat a tablespoon of oil in a large frying pan over a high heat, then ladle 2 tablespoons of the batter into the pan. After a minute or so, when the pancake is golden underneath, use a slice to turn it over. The other side should brown very quickly. Remove it from the pan and place on a plate. Add a little more oil to the pan and repeat until all the batter is used up.

- Serve with the reserved apples and a little maple syrup, or if you have a really sweet tooth try golden syrup.

Save time … by weighing and mixing all the dry ingredients before bedtime, so pancakes can be served only 10 minutes after waking in the morning.

Try … swapping the apples for blueberries if you happen to have them in the fridge/freezer. You can keep the pancakes warm in a low oven, separated by non-stick baking paper, so everyone can eat breakfast (or dessert!) together.

Iceland

Lemon Tart

Everyone should have a reliable recipe for this classic 'little black dress' of a dessert. You can dress this down by serving it with a little vanilla ice cream or dress it up with crème fraîche and fresh raspberries soaked in framboise liqueur.

For the pastry
250g plain flour
50g icing sugar
125g cold butter, cut into cubes
1 large egg, beaten

For the filling
5 large eggs, at room temperature
150ml double cream
200g caster sugar
juice and zest of 3 lemons

For decorating
icing sugar

To prepare 1 hour | **To cook** 35 minutes | **Serves** 12

- Mix together the flour and icing sugar in a large bowl. Rub in the butter using your thumbs and fingertips to create a breadcrumb-like consistency. Add the beaten egg and stir it in with a blunt knife to bind the mixture together.

- Lightly flour the work surface and roll the pastry to a thickness of about 3mm using a floured rolling pin. Have ready a 28cm loose-bottomed tart tin. Slip both hands under the pastry with palms facing upwards and fingers spread wide, move it over the tin and lower it into place. Push the pastry gently into the bottom of the tin, then run the rolling pin over the edges to trim the pastry level with the tin. Chill for 30 minutes.

- Preheat the oven to 190°C/Fan 170°C/Gas Mark 5. Line the pastry, including the sides, with a circle of non-stick baking paper and fill it with baking beans or uncooked rice or pulses. Bake in the oven for 12 minutes until the edges are just beginning to brown, then remove the beans and paper and bake for a further 5 minutes. Remove from the oven and turn the oven down to 160°C/Fan 140°C/Gas Mark 3.

- Prepare the filling by whisking all the ingredients together for 2 minutes until they look creamy and well combined, then transfer the mixture to a jug for easy pouring. Place the pastry case back into the oven with the shelf sticking out a little, and very carefully pour the lemony filling into the case, being careful not to spill any down the sides of the pastry.

- Very gently push the shelf back into the oven, close the door and let the tart bake for 15–20 minutes until the filling has set but has a tiny wobble in the middle. Remove from the oven and leave to cool on a wire rack at room temperature for 4 hours. Dust with icing sugar just before serving.

- The tart will keep, refrigerated, for 3 days.

Save time ... by defrosting a 500g block of ready-made shortcrust pastry rather than making your own. Form any offcuts into biscuit shapes and sprinkle with icing sugar once cool – waste not, want not!

Try ... serving the tart with a grating of white chocolate, along with a shot of limoncello on the side.

Popcorn Caramel Cheesecake

This no-bake cheesecake takes the humble cinema snack to a whole new level with the power of homemade caramel.

For the base

120g digestive biscuits, crushed (about 8 biscuits)
75g butter, melted
1 tablespoon caster sugar

For the cheesecake

180g cream cheese, softened
50g icing sugar
1 teaspoon vanilla extract
184ml double cream, whipped to stiff peaks

For the topping

100g salted butter
120g dark brown sugar
100ml double cream
1 teaspoon vanilla extract
60g sweet popcorn

To prepare 45 minutes | **To chill** 4 hours | **Serves** 12

- Grease and line a 20cm springform cake tin with cling film – this is important as it makes the cheesecake much easier to remove later. Mix the biscuits, melted butter and sugar together then press this into the tin using the back of a metal spoon. Chill in the fridge for 10 minutes.

- To make the cheesecake layer, beat the cream cheese, icing sugar and vanilla extract with an electric mixer or a wooden spoon until combined. Gently fold through the whipped double cream using a large metal spoon and spoon the filling on to the chilled biscuit base. Smooth until flat, leaving a slight ridge around the edge (this helps the caramel sauce to stay on top of the cheesecake) and chill for 2 hours.

- Meanwhile, make the caramel. Melt the butter in a medium saucepan over a low heat. Add the brown sugar and whisk well. Once the sugar has dissolved slightly and looks less grainy, add the cream, stir and turn up the heat. As soon as the mixture comes to a boil, reduce the heat and cook at a low simmer for 5 minutes, stirring all the time (it's best to time this stage as you need to be precise). The mixture will bubble and spit a little as it's simmering, so be careful not to stand too close and make sure children aren't near the hob. After 5 minutes, remove from the heat and add the vanilla extract – beware, the mixture will bubble up again. Then stir and leave the caramel to thicken and cool.

- When the caramel is thick, at room temperature, but still pourable, reserve 3 tablespoons, then spoon the rest over the top of the chilled cheesecake. Add the popcorn and drizzle the remaining 3 tablespoons of caramel on top. Chill for another 2 hours.

- **NOTE** You can make this cheesecake the night before you need it, but make the caramel and popcorn topping on the day.

Save time ... use a ready-made toffee or caramel sauce rather than making your own. It won't be as thick, so drizzle it over the cheesecake portions after slicing.

Try ... toasting some pecans or hazelnuts to finely chop and add to the biscuit base. Or add ½ teaspoon of salt to the caramel and use salted popcorn rather than sweet for a salted caramel version.

Iceland

Iceland

Revel® Roulette Brownies

*Squidgy chocolate brownies studded with Revels®.
It's all down to luck as to whether you get
a coffee one or an orange one!*

325g dark chocolate, not more than
   40% cocoa solids
125g salted butter
150g caster sugar
90g soft brown sugar
3 large eggs
100g plain flour
1 x 126g bag Revels®

To prepare 20 minutes | **To cook** 30 minutes | **Makes** 9 large brownies or 16 smaller ones – cut them as small as you wish

- Grease and line a 20 x 30cm baking tray with non-stick baking paper and preheat the oven to 180°C/Fan 160°C/Gas Mark 4.

- Break the chocolate into squares and melt, together with the butter, in a large saucepan over a very low heat, stirring regularly to ensure that the chocolate doesn't burn. Remove from the heat when smooth and add the sugars, eggs and flour. Stir well until smooth.

- Pour half of the batter into the tray. Scatter the Revels® on top and then pour over the rest of the batter, ensuring that all the Revels® are covered (if they do poke through, they have a tendency to burn a little in the oven).

- Bake for 25–30 minutes until the brownie has stopped wobbling and is starting to look a little cracked at the edges. Cool (still in the pan) on a wire rack and refrigerate for an hour, then cut with a sharp knife.

Save time ... by using chocolate chips so you don't have to break up the chocolate. They'll melt faster too.

Save money ... by making plain brownies without the Revels® – they're still delicious!

Try ... experimenting with different chocolate, use your favourite chopped up instead of Revels® – Mars Bars® are very good!

Iceland

Cinnamon Apple Galette

This is a lazy person's apple pie, but with no compromise on flavour. With a galette (which is basically a free-form pie) there's no need for lining pie dishes or complicated crimping. This galette is delicious either served warm or cold the next day.

For the pastry

125g cold butter (salted or unsalted, whatever you have to hand)
250g plain flour, plus extra for rolling
1 large egg

For the filling

15ml lemon juice
480g peeled, cored and thinly sliced apples (7 small apples)
75g raisins
¼ teaspoon ground cinnamon
15g plain flour
45g granulated sugar

To glaze

1 egg, whisked lightly with a pinch of salt to form an egg wash
2 teaspoons granulated sugar

To prepare 20 minutes plus chilling I **To cook** 45 minutes I **Serves** 6

• Make the pastry. Rub the butter into the flour to a fine breadcrumb consistency (or blitz in a food processor with the blade attachment), then use the egg to bind the pastry. Either stir in with a blunt knife or pulse in short bursts in the food processor until the pastry just starts to gather into clumps. Stop stirring/processing at this point and gather up with your hands. Shape the pastry into a disc, wrap in cling film and chill for 1 hour.

• Prepare the filling by stirring everything together; cover and chill for 40 minutes or until the pastry is chilled.

• Preheat the oven to 190°C/Fan 170°C/Gas Mark 5 and line a baking tray with non-stick baking paper. Roll the disc of pastry out on a floured work surface using a floured rolling pin to about 3mm thickness and in a rough circle shape about 35cm in diameter. Move it gently to the prepared baking tray. Pile the apple filling into the middle. Be careful not to pour it all in, as you don't want to include any syrup left at the bottom of the bowl, for fear of a soggy bottom.

• Fold the pastry edges into the centre, leaving the middle of the apples exposed. Be careful not to let the pastry break as you do this (if it does, use your fingers to push any cracks back together). Finally, egg-wash the pastry all over using a pastry brush and sprinkle the whole galette with sugar. Bake for 45 minutes until the pastry is golden brown and the apples have started to caramelise on the top.

• Serve warm with ice cream, cream or custard.

Save time ... by using ready–made shortcrust pastry.

Try ... adding grated marzipan to the filling for a festive version; or add a few pecans instead. For a more adult dessert, try soaking the raisins in brandy for 10 minutes before you begin assembling the pie.

Iceland

Iceland

Speedy Chocolate Berry Steamed Pudding

This is a dangerous recipe to have in the house; you're basically only ever 15 minutes away from a very naughty chocolatey steamed pudding. No mixer required, just stir it all up with a fork and off you go.

55g butter
15g golden syrup
55g soft dark brown sugar
10g cocoa
1 large egg
80g self-raising flour
2 tablespoons milk
30g mixed berries, frozen or fresh

To prepare 5 minutes | **To cook** 5 minutes plus standing | **Serves** 2–4

- Take a microwavable cereal-sized bowl (at least 9cm high and 8cm across), place the butter in it and microwave on 'medium' for 1 minute or until the butter has melted; add the syrup and stir.

- Add the rest of the ingredients, apart from the berries, and whisk with a fork for 2 minutes until smooth and well combined.

- Stir in the mixed berries and microwave for 5 minutes on 'high', without a lid, until the pudding is well risen. Remove from the microwave and allow to stand for 5 minutes before serving. Be careful – the berries will still be piping hot.

- This pudding is best served warm. If you do eat it cold, then serve with pouring cream, ice cream or custard to counteract any dryness that microwave puddings can be prone to upon cooling.

Save time ... by weighing out all the ingredients before you serve dinner so there's no extra waiting around for dessert.

Try ... using different fruits. Blueberries would work well. You could even make an impromptu Black Forest gateau with a cherry version by serving with whipped double cream and lots of chocolate shavings.

Chocolate and Peanut Oaty Cookies

These buttery, oaty cookies are full of peanuts and chocolate. They're perfect with a hot cup of tea or an ice-cold glass of milk and have a habit of disappearing very quickly.

110g very soft, salted butter
70g caster sugar
60g soft light brown sugar
1 large egg, at room temperature
1 teaspoon bicarbonate of soda
135g self-raising flour
70g crunchy peanut butter
160g porridge oats
100g salted peanuts
200g chocolate chips or dark chocolate,
   cut into chunks

To prepare 25 minutes I **To cook** 15 minutes I **Makes** about 20

- Preheat the oven to 180°C/Fan 160°C/Gas Mark 4 and line 3 baking trays with non-stick baking paper.

- Cream the butter and sugars together until light and creamy using a wooden spoon. Add the egg, mix well and then add all the other ingredients and mix until just combined.

- Scoop golf ball-sized pieces of dough on to the lined trays, spacing them at least 5cm apart to allow for spreading, squash them a little with a fork to about 1.5cm high. Bake for 10–15 minutes until browned and cracked on the surface.

- If you like a brittle cookie, bake until very dark brown. If you like a chewy-centred cookie, then bake until just blushed with a tan. Cool on the trays before transferring to a cookie tin.

Save time ... by making this cookie dough up to 2 days before you use it. Just form into a sausage shape, wrap in cling film and keep in the fridge. Cut circles of the mixture and bake from chilled. You can freeze the sausage instead if you like. Defrost overnight in the fridge before using.

Try ... serving two cookies sandwiched together with vanilla ice cream for a decadent dessert that's more than a little messy to eat.

Iceland

Iceland

Index

Iceland

Iceland

Conversion Charts

Weights

Metric	Imperial
15g	½oz
25g	1oz
40g	1½oz
50g	2oz
60g	2½oz
75g	3oz
100g	3½oz
125g	4oz
150g	5oz
175g	6oz
200g	7oz
225g	8oz
250g	9oz
275g	10oz
300g	11oz
350g	12oz
375g	13oz
400g	14oz
425g	1lb
500g	1lb 2oz
650g	1lb 7oz
675g	1½lb
700g	1lb 9oz
750g	1lb 11oz
900g	2lb
1kg	2lb 4oz
1.5kg	3lb 6oz

Volumes

Metric	Imperial
25ml	1fl oz
50ml	2fl oz
75ml	3fl oz
100ml	4fl oz
150ml	5fl oz (¼ pint)
175ml	6fl oz
200ml	7fl oz
225ml	8fl oz
250ml	9fl oz
300ml	10fl oz (½ pint)
350ml	13fl oz
400ml	14fl oz
450ml	16fl oz (¾ pint)
600ml	20fl oz (1 pint)
750ml	25fl oz (1¼ pints)
900ml	30fl oz (1½ pints)
1 litre	34fl oz (1¾ pints)
1.2 litres	40fl oz (2 pints)
1.5 litres	52fl oz (2½ pints)
1.8 litres	60fl oz (3 pints)

Iceland

Measurements

Milimeters	Inches
2mm	¹⁄₁₆in
3mm	⅛ in
4mm	⅙ in
5mm	¼ in
1cm	½in
2cm	¾ in
2.5cm	1in
3cm	1¼in
4cm	1½in
4.5cm	1¾in
5cm	2in
6cm	2½in
7.5cm	3in
9cm	3½in
10cm	4in
13cm	5in
13.5cm	5¼in
15cm	6in
16cm	6½in
18cm	7in
19cm	7½in
20cm	8in
23cm	9in
24cm	9½in
25.5cm	10in
28cm	11in
30cm	12in
32.5cm	13in
35cm	14in
37.5cm	15in

Oven Temperatures

Conventional	Fan	Gas
110°c	90°c	-
120°c	100°c	½
140°c	120°c	1
150°c	130°c	2
160°c	140°c	3
180°c	160°c	4
190°c	170°c	5
200°c	180°c	6
220°c	200°c	7
230°c	210°c	8
240°c	220°c	9

Iceland

About the Author

I know there's no such thing as a 'normal mum' but that's how I, and many women I know, describe ourselves. I'm a stay-at-home mum who sometimes loves her 'job' and sometimes wants to tear her hair out. I'm like every other mum across the country: not enough time, pulled a thousand ways, often feeling happy, sometimes feeling guilty, trying my best to bring up my little brood. It's both the best and the hardest job in the world. And food and feeding are a huge part of any mum or dad's role as chief nurturer.

What else can I tell you about me? I spent a year studying midwifery in my late teens and so have delivered ten babies. I studied English Language and Literature at the University in Liverpool. I spent my 20's living in London and working in advertising. I met my husband back at home in Leicester one Christmas and nine days after our first meeting he proposed. We have three sons, Charlie, 6, Max, 4 and Lawrence, 1.

In 2011 I competed and finished as a finalist in BBC2's *Great British Bake Off*. It was both amazing and stressful all at the same time, a truly unique experience where I learnt that I am far more resilient than I thought, that you can make a friend for life in just six weeks and that forgetting to tick off the ingredients for a recipe can result in one hell of a tasteless sponge!

And since then so much has happened. I have been able to leave the world of advertising behind and make my living from food through recipe writing, blogging (www.recipesfromanormalmum.com), presenting and teaching.

And of course I'm thrilled to be working with Iceland. I've always loved frozen food. My husband poked fun at me very early on in our relationship when I berated him for not using his freezer effectively. It was virtually empty (save some ice and a few sausages that had seen better days)! It wasn't long before I'd filled it with Iceland frozen goodies, homemade frozen berry yoghurt lollies and pizza kits.

And the best thing about this recipe book? All the profits go to the Children's Food Trust. There's pretty much nothing I feel more passionately about than feeding the next generation well. So, thank you for buying this book, and do let me and Iceland know which recipes are your favourites.

🐦 @IcelandFoods
📘 Iceland Foods
📷 @IcelandFoods

🐦 @HollyBellMummy
📘 Recipes from a Normal Mum
📷 @HollyBellMummy